Asian Arguments

Asian Arguments is a series of short books about Asia today. Aimed at the growing number of students and general readers who want to know more about the region, these books will highlight community involvement from the ground up in issues of the day usually discussed by authors in terms of top-down government policy. The aim is to better understand how ordinary Asian citizens are confronting problems such as the environment, democracy and their societies' development, either with or without government support. The books are scholarly but engaged, substantive as well as topical, and written by authors with direct experience of their subject matter.

SERIES EDITOR Paul French

Related titles in Asian Arguments

ALREADY PUBLISHED

China's Urban Billion by Tom Miller
China and the Environment edited by Sam Geall
Leftover Women by Leta Hong Fincher
North Korea: State of Paranoia by Paul French

FORTHCOMING

Kashgar by Sam Chambers
The Enemy Within by Francis Wade
Myanmar by Irene Slight and Simon Long
Out of Pol Pot's Shadow by Christina Larson
Last Days of the Mighty Mekong by Brian Eyler

About the author

Wade Shepard is an itinerant writer who has been travelling the world since 1999. He grew up in western New York State, at the heart of the infamous Rust Belt – a place that knows ghost cities well. Having graduated from Long Island University Global (then Friends World Program), he has made his living as an archaeologist, a geographical researcher, a journalist, a farmhand and an independent blogger. In 2005 he ended up in China for the first time, and he hasn't been able to fully shake the country yet. Wade is a contributor to the *South China Morning Post*; his work also appears in other major China-focused publications. He blogs at Vagabondjourney.com. For more on China's ghost cities visit Ghostcitiesofchina.com.

Ghost Cities of China

THE STORY OF CITIES WITHOUT PEOPLE IN THE WORLD'S MOST POPULATED COUNTRY

Wade Shepard

Zed Books

LONDON

Ghost Cities of China: The Story of Cities without People in the World's Most Populated Country was first published in 2015 by Zed Books Ltd, 7 Cynthia Street, London N1 9JF, UK

www.zedbooks.co.uk

Typeset in Monotype Bulmer by illuminati, Grosmont
Index by John Barker
Cover design www.stevenmarsden.com

A catalogue record for this book is available from the British Library

ISBN 978-1-78360-219-3 hb
ISBN 978-1-78360-218-6 pb
ISBN 978-1-78360-220-9 pdf
ISBN 978-1-78360-221-6 epub
ISBN 978-1-78360-222-3 mobi

Printed and bound by CPI Group (UK) Ltd, Croydon, CR0 4YY

Contents

Acknowledgements

I was once a freewheeling, light-hearted blogger who travelled the world, investigating any intrigue that struck my fancy, writing about whatever I wanted, and working for myself alone. I took assignments from no editor. I ran a team of ten writers where I called the shots and distributed the assignments. I was independent and proud. Then Paul French wrote: 'Wade, Just writing on the off chance that you might be interested in turning your series of articles on China's ghost towns and French/German Towns etc. into a small book for a series I edit called Asian Arguments for Zed Books in London.'

I responded with a 'Definitely, yes', before I'd even finished reading the email. Apparently, my maverick resolve was not as robust as I'd assumed.

Throughout the year that followed I continued chasing down ghost cities and new developments across China, working arduously on assembling a manuscript on a topic that seemed to be changing faster than I could put down words about it. At every step of the way there were people who helped, directly or indirectly, to make *Ghost Cities of China* happen. I owe much gratitude to Kim Walker, my commissioning editor at Zed, for taking a shot on a first-time author and showing me the ropes of formal publishing. Thank you to Justin O'Jack, whose example, lessons and encouragement always made me feel that I could really accomplish something here in China. Thank you to Andy Graham of HoboTraveler.com, who long ago scooped me out of the mire of bloggers and showed me the path. Thank you to Patricia Franck Sheffield, whose letters of encouragement and support kept me walking in the footsteps of her father, the 'King of Vagabonds'. Thank you to Steve Mendoza, who was there at the beginning, pouring me beers and politely listening to my incessant monologues about the nuances of urban development. I owe a debt of gratitude to the Friends World Program (now Global College) of Long Island University that extends far beyond my defaulted student loans – your school for itinerant eccentrics taught me how to do things like conduct research in places like China. Thank you to the Maine family, Erik Pike, Donald Herbert, my sisters Nicky and Meili, and all the old friends from the fields and orchards of Western New York. Thanks to my mother and father, who never lost their sense of pride in their only son and brainwashed him into believing that he could accomplish whatever he dreamed up. And, of course, thank you to Paul French, who may have broken the inertia of my independence but in the process gave me that proverbial 'break'.

Soon after I began this book I discovered that an author rarely works alone. There are often people behind the scenes picking up the slack and handling the mundane affairs of the world of dust while we play around in our literary la-la lands. I have been led to believe that these people are as essential to the book-writing process as pads of paper, voice recorders, Evernote and Scrivener, and I was fortunate enough to have one of these indispensable characters for myself. When I emptied my bank account rushing thousands of miles across China to gawk at barren construction sites and demolished villages, there was someone back home who paid the rent. When I sat hypnotized by the computer screen for hour after hour, day after day, there was someone doing the dishes, sweeping the floor and shopping for groceries. When I was too busy to make food, there was someone there to feed me. When I was stomping through cities without people, there was someone at home, doing a real job and taking care of my daughter. I will take the credit, the cheers and the jeers for the book that follows, but none of it would have been possible without the continuous support of the invisible hand that held it all together: my wife, Hannah Chaya. This book is dedicated to you. For a MacArthur and National Medal of Science-winning geographer's granddaughter you suspended all reason, ignored the empirical evidence and abandoned common sense to believe in this squalid, prospect-deficient *goy*. They told you that you were crazy; you readily agreed, but you stuck it out anyway. Thank you.

This book is also for Motorcycle Bob Lyskowski, Deb Goss and the rest of the supporters of VagabondJourney.com – you showed up in the early days and just kept reading, every step of the way, saying 'You know, you should really write a book.' Well, I did write a book, but it may not have happened without all of you who never permitted me the luxury to quit. Walk Slow.

Preface

As I walked I could hear myself breathing, I could hear my boots hitting concrete, the wind blowing, and little else. It's the silence that makes China's ghost cities so startling. It's not just the deficit of people, but the fact that sound waves just become lost in the extensive empty space between buildings, across streets, and over barren construction lots. You can watch the scant few people there are cycling or driving cars but essentially hear nothing. This feeling of vertigo is compounded by the fact that everything in these places appears so familiar, yet seems so unreal. There are skyscrapers, high-rises, shopping malls, boulevards and parks, but the absence of masses of humanity pouring through them makes it all seem like a life-sized version of the little plastic scale models of cities that are proudly displayed in the offices of architecture firms. There is something about these places that your senses detect as being false, like a basket of plastic fruit sitting before the easel of an art student painting a still life, but your rationale tells you that it is all very much for real.

I wouldn't be telling the full truth if I claimed that my interest in China's ghost cities was purely journalistic. I grew up in the Great Lakes region of the USA between Buffalo and Rochester, New York – right in the heart of the all too accurately named 'Rust Belt'. This is an area that knows ghost cities well. In my early twenties I would spend my weekends going out to the abandoned factory towns. I would walk through the completely deserted neighbourhoods of Lackawanna, break into the decommissioned mills that line Buffalo's waterfront, sneak around in the abandoned factories of Rochester. The appeal was the real potential for seeing something unexpected and out of the ordinary, the thrill of surprise – and I was more often than not given incredible doses of both. But the real intrigue was the stimulation of dreaming about how these once great and prosperous places descended into decadence and ruin.

It was the starkly ephemeral that got me. It was the feeling that time is always rolling on and the sure-shot guarantee that the huge amounts of energy, resources and manpower being pumped into the great works of today will ultimately produce the rubble heaps of tomorrow. Everything is born and everything dies – even cities. In my home region of Western New York I was able to grow accustomed to places that had perished; in China I became familiar with those that were just being born. The effect of each was similar – places hovering in stagnancy with diminutive populations and scant levels of activity – but the questions I asked myself were radically different. While in the post-industrial wastelands of Buffalo and Rochester I would wonder what had happened and what was, in the new cities of China my fascination was framed in another grammatical tense: what is going to happen and what will be?

There is a thrill to travelling to China's new cities. As in an abandoned Rust Belt factory, you don't know what you're going to find in them. You never know what is going to be around the next corner, down the dusty halls of the next deserted shopping mall, or up the next half-built skyscraper. Many of these places are not even on the map yet; the most recent satellite imagery is already outdated, still showing them to be villages or empty construction lots. When you go to one of China's big new urban developments you know that there is a chance that you may be in one of the world's next landmark cities, staring upon what will soon become a hub of commerce and trade, though you also know that you may be in the pre-emptive ruins of the next white elephant. Either prospect is exhilarating, and to see these places now is to take away a mnemonic snapshot from the summit of a social, political and economic upheaval like the world has never known before. What side of the slope China's new cities will roll down will define the country's future and impact the world. Right now only one thing is certain: something big is happening here.

China's ghost cities also presented me with another intrigue. I've been moving through the world since 1999, visiting and living in fifty or so countries before finding myself netted within the giant expanse of China a few years ago. There is often a subdued, archaic thirst in the traveller to be the first to make it to a place, to be the first one to chart out a new dot on the map and then return home to tell everyone about it. Though the age of discovery has long been over and done, the explorer's conceit is still with us. While most of the places in this world are known globally, their locations marked by GPS, their terrains photographed via satellite, and their streets crawling with tourists, China has presented the passé wanderer with a loophole: new cities – hundreds of them. While it's safe to assume that more or less every new large-scale development in China has already attracted teams of foreign planners, designers and builders, not many outside of this professional realm have actually visited these places, let alone have written about them. I have to admit here that I found it appealing to research places that have not yet been thoroughly described, photographed and conceptually nailed down. Rather than racing to be the first to discover locales lost, forgotten and obscured, the new game was to witness and describe places that were just being created.

China's new cities are just that: new. They are still rising above the ground, rapidly transcending entropy to create order. Where else in the world could I walk through an entire city that was being built all around me? Where else could I stroll down a wide dirt boulevard surrounded by half-constructed skyscrapers in every direction? When else would I have the opportunity to see the locations of what would become booming metropolises before they even exist? We tend to think of cities as permanent entities, as though they were always there. But that is never the case. All cities rise and all cities fall, but the opportunity for anyone to be in the exact place at the exact time that either happens is rare. China provided me with this opportunity in spades. For two years I observed the rampant spread of urbanization; I talked with the city builders as they worked. I've watched towns and villages grow into metropolises; I've learned what the transition between rural and urban – the fundamental dividing line of humanity leading back to the dawn of civilization – is really like. For two years I watched places become.

While my ghost city research was ultimately for professional purposes, I must admit here that a good deal of the allure was personal.

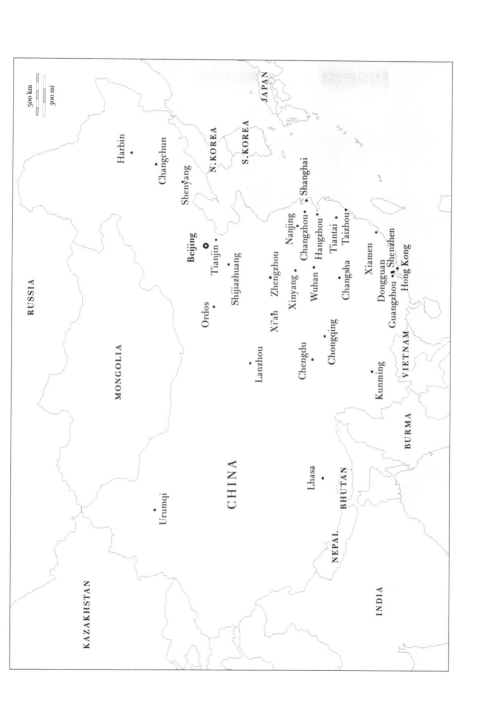

ONE

The new map of China

It is projected that by 2030 one in eight people on earth will live in a Chinese city (Miller 2012). Preparation for this deluge is reshaping the country. Hundreds of new districts, cities, towns and neighbourhoods are being constructed as hundreds of millions of Chinese are expected to transition from rural to urban terrains. China has designed a master urbanization plan unlike anything ever seen before in history, but its implementation has produced a peculiar side effect: ghost cities, everywhere.

These empty new cities, dubbed 'ghost towns' by the international media, have became a global phenomenon and a major point of confusion and contention among China watchers, journalists, governmental agencies and investors alike. One common point of view is that these stagnant new cities reveal a crack in the veneer of the rising superpower, that China's staggering GDP and economic ascension really isn't all it's said to be, that decades of irresponsibly rampant development and growth are now taking their toll. These claims posit China's ghost cities as harbingers of a premature collapse of the country, which could produce a ripple that takes the entire global economy down along with it. Headlines like 'China's property slowdown could have a domino effect on global commodities' play on the fear of a Western readership that is already primed to be on edge about China. Whatever the case, the reports of new cities with wide open, empty streets, block upon block of vacant buildings, and entire skyscrapers with nobody in them have caught the imagination of the world. But it quickly becomes apparent that beneath the thin veil of sensationalism very little is actually known about China's ghost cities.

In 2006, I stepped out of a bus station into what I initially took to be the downtown area of Tiantai, a small city in the mountains of Zhejiang province. As I walked in search of a hotel I did not notice at first the ominous fact that every building was completely vacant and that I was the only person on the streets. The realization came as a shock, and I stopped immediately and gazed at the brand new, grey-tiled five-storey buildings that surrounded me. They were identical, like a matching suite of furniture. The shops and hotels and homes were all skeletal frames of what they were intended to become. Outside, they appeared to be crisp and new; inside, they were dark cavities, devoid of inhabitants, users, or even any interior fit-out. The buildings, streets, parks and public squares were all woven together as a part of a singular urban design that was propelled into existence by a singular blast of construction. It was a planned city, a place that was designed on computers, projected onto screens in boardrooms, and made into little plastic scale renders before being replicated in real life upon the loamy river valley soil of Tiantai.

This was long before the first ghost city reports came out, so I had no solid reference for what I was looking at. What was this place? How did this happen? Where did all the people go? Were they ever here at all? It was as though a giant vacuum cleaner had hovered overhead and all signs of life had been sucked up like dust, leaving behind nothing but bare grey infrastructure. It took me over an hour of walking through the barren maze of buildings before I realized that the inhabited part of the city lay a couple of kilometres down the road, that I was in the new part of town that was built but not inhabited.

I was a student at Zhejiang University at the time. When I returned I told my professors about what I had observed, with no small dose of immature excitement. They just looked at me, shrugged uninterestedly, and said, 'Yeah, those places are everywhere.' Chinese academics were apparently aware of my discovery, but they weren't interested.

However, there was something about the phrase 'those places are everywhere' that kept me locked onto the topic. Later that year I stumbled off a highway into a deserted portion of Erenhot on the Mongolian border, a place that would later gain infamy through the ghost city reports that the Western media were soon to publish about it. As I walked through that sand-strewn, completely empty new city that was flung out in the Gobi Desert it became clear that something very big was happening here. What were insignificant small cities like Tiantai and Erenhot doing building entire new districts that essentially doubled their size? Why weren't there any people or businesses in these places? What was all of this for? What would become of this? Only one thing was certain at that point: these places really were everywhere.

The ghost city critique

In 2009, Al Jazeera's Melissa Chan claimed to have stumbled into Ordos Kangbashi by mistake when reporting on another story, and the world was introduced to China's ghost cities. Since then, many international news programmes, such as *Dateline Australia* and *60 Minutes*, have ventured into a well-chosen small sample of China's new cities, declared them ghost towns, and established the dominant angle of the international media: 'If building a road pumped up GDP, then building a whole city would really propel GDP growth to unknown heights' (Chan 2011).

Suddenly, places such as Erenhot, Zhengdong, Chenggong, Dantu, Xinyang and Linyi were put on the map. These reports showed the empty buildings, the deserted streets, the stillborn carcasses of cities that never knew life. These places were decried as failures, evidence that China has been rigging the books on its remarkable GDP growth, and as an ominous sign that the country's rampant pace of development has finally caught up with it. These reports helped plant a seed of suspicion that the rise of China may not be as touted and that the world's fledgling superpower was building cities for nobody. But was this true?

So I again began tracking down new cities – or ghost cities, as they were now called – across China. All I had to do was take a bus to the edge of a city, get off, and look. Invariably, there would be a new town under construction. For the following two years I was out in the streets, or dirt paths as they sometimes were, of half-built new cities, talking to their builders, interviewing their designers, interrogating their investors, and meeting their residents – if there were any. I wanted to know what these new places were being built for, who would come and live in them, what life would be like there, and what their future would be. What I found was a movement that's physically and figuratively reshaping China and, by extension, the world.

Building a new world within the four seas

'Around fourteen years ago I went up into that tower with an urban developer and we looked south', a German contractor in Taizhou, Jiangsu told me. 'We could see all the way to the river then; there was nothing in between. The developer then pointed into the distance and said that he was building a city there. Now there's a city.' This is perhaps the quintessential narrative of early-twenty-first-century China.

When the Communist Party assumed power in 1949 China had 69 cities; today it has 658. This is a country that seems like one colossal, ever-churning construction site. The old is being replaced with the new, and the new is being replaced with the newer, in a cyclical process of creation and destruction. The ensemble of jackhammers, cranes, dump trucks and sledgehammers is the soundtrack of a country reinventing itself. Like an architect sketching on a drawing board, massive swathes of land are being cleared of buildings and inhabitants and entire new cities are going up in their place. Over the next twenty years China will build hundreds of new cities, thousands of new towns and districts, erect over 50,000 new skyscrapers, wipe untold thousands of villages off the map, and relocate hundreds of millions of people in a development boom that's incomparable in scale and scope to anything we've yet seen. No civilization has ever built so much so quickly.

Nearly 600 new cities have already been established across China in roughly sixty-five years, and there is no sign of a slowdown yet. According to a 2013 survey conducted by China's National Development and Reform Commission, it was found that 144 cities in just twelve of China's thirty-two provincial-level areas were in the process of building over 200 new towns. Nationwide, new urban developments are popping up faster than surveys can be conducted to count them. This means that nearly every city in the country is expanding – some are doubling or even tripling their size. It is no wonder that China uses 40 per cent of the world's supply of cement and steel. The amount of cement the country used in the last three years alone tops what the United States used during the entire twentieth century. This is in a country that is already home to a quarter of the world's hundred largest cities and has 171 municipalities with over a million people in each.

These new cities and urban expansions are not just being built at random off the grid. Rather, all of this urbanization is advancing within the tight frame of an expansive new transportation network. Layered grids of new highways and high-speed rail lines are being stretched across the country, new subways are being dug beneath most major cities, and, above it all, the air transport nexus is growing exponentially. By 2020 forty Chinese cities will have subway systems, totalling 7,000 km of track – over five times the total of the USA. In 2005, China had 41,000 km of highway; in just nine years this had multiplied by two and a half times and is now the most extensive network in the world. Prior to 2003 China had no high-speed rail lines in operation; it now has a system that totals 12,000 km, the most extensive in the world, which is expected to grow to 50,000 km by 2020 – enough to stretch around the world one and a quarter times. On top of this, 82 new civil airports are being built and 101 current airports are being expanded. This includes a US$14 billion behemoth in the south of Beijing that will be the size of Bermuda and will require 116,000 people to be relocated. By the end of 2015, 80 per cent of the Chinese population will live within 100 km of an airport. To prevent the new city movement from running away with itself, China is corralling it all in with infrastructure – although, at US$163 million per kilometre of new subway track (Qi 2014), in excess of US$300 billion for the high-speed rail network, US$240 billion for the highway system, and hundreds of billions of dollars for the new airports, this doesn't come cheap.

This urban transition, of course, isn't just a matter of constructing new buildings and infrastructure, as there is also a drastic social upheaval under way. In 1949, just 12 per cent of China's population lived in cities; today that number is up to more than half of the population, totalling 731 million people. Within the past thirty years 400 million Chinese, more than the entire population of the United States, have transitioned from rural to urban areas; throughout the first decade of the twenty-first century the country's urban head count was growing by the population of Australia annually. But China's not done yet. By governmental decree, 300 million more people are expected to become urban by 2030, the much portended year when the country is expected to have 1 billion city dwellers. This means that 1.4 million Chinese, roughly the population of Estonia, will need to urbanize each month for the next sixteen years.

As I take in all of these facts about China's urbanization movement, it seems so incredible as to be abstract and somewhat unreal. The massive numbers blur into meaninglessness, and the sheer scale of what is being built seems to defy comprehension. How large actually is a 500-square-kilometre new district? What does laying 12,000 km of new high-speed rail lines across an entire country really involve? What do these hundreds of new cities look like? The book that follows chronicles two years of travelling around China investigating the country's new city movement. It covers how sites are selected for development and the mass evictions and relocations which ensue; how new cities are built and the strategies that are used to populate them; how the rural poor are flooding into urban areas and how policies have been created to bring cities to the countryside; how China is financing its urbanization movement and the pitfalls within its fiscal system that make excessive overdevelopment an inevitability; how there is a master plan in place that will soon blanket the country in a web of megacity clusters; and why, in the world's most populated country, there are entire cities without people.

TWO

Clearing the land

I was walking in the middle of the street near the central core of the world's most populated city, but I had no fear of being run over, honked at or knocked aside. There was no traffic; the only cars were a row of black Lexuses sitting idly on the sidewalk outside a monolithic exhibition centre, their bored chauffeurs smoking cigarettes and playing with their phones. The wind was blowing gently, the sun was shining, and the magpies were squawking. Landmark skyscrapers, colossal bridges and roaring highways formed a ring around me, but where I was standing was all calm and quiet, the raucous soundtrack of the city was dulled to a quiet, static-like hum. I was in the hole of an urban donut, Shanghai's World Expo site: a dead zone close to the centre of the city.

It wasn't always like this. This was once an area of factories, naval bases, ports and neighbourhoods which flanked the banks of the Huangpu River as it snakes through the heart of Shanghai. This place was destined for redevelopment at some point, being just a tick upriver from Pudong's Lujiazui Central Business District; it was the arrival of a temporary exposition that provided the local government with the impetus to pull the trigger.

The 2010 World Expo was Shanghai's response to Beijing's 2008 Olympics, and was supposed to have been the event that catapulted it to the status of 'next great world city'. At a cost of

US$58.58 billion, roughly the annual GDP of Croatia, the city used the Expo as the justification for a complete makeover. Ten years of planning and preparation went into event, which saw six new subway lines dug, the addition of 4,000 new taxis, a new airport terminal, the second longest steel-arch bridge in the world, and myriad other urban renewal projects. For the Expo site itself, a 5.82 sq km site, the size of a thousand soccer fields, was chosen just to the south of Shanghai's downtown, which spanned both sides of the Huangpu River. To access this swathe of land, 18,452 households and 270 factories had to be cleared away. They were hustled off to the outskirts.

The people who previously lived at the Expo site were forced to relocate, their homes demolished and trucked away. Many claim to have been given minimal compensation; some became homeless. Those who complained too loudly were detained. 'My house was on the main site of the Expo', a Mr Han told a reporter for the *Daily Telegraph*. 'They waited until we left home one day and then knocked it down. I have not had any payment for my property and, because I complained, my son was refused entrance to university and then to the army. I am unemployed, and so is my wife and my son. We live on the bare minimum, around 500 yuan (£47) a month' (Moore 2010). Protests over these evictions erupted in Shanghai, Taiwan, and at the UN's headquarters in New York. Some 1,000 evicted residents marched in Beijing. Shen Ting of the League of Chinese Victims, a human rights advocacy group, asked rhetorically: 'What has the Shanghai World Expo brought to the residents of Shanghai? We say it is pain, tears, despair and uncertainty.' A total of 38 human rights groups urged the UN to investigate potential human rights abuses, but it didn't heed the call. Instead, the UN built a 32,000-square-foot pavilion to 'present a positive image of the UN family' and the secretary general, Ban Ki-moon, lauded the Chinese government and Shanghai.

For the event itself, Shanghai was sure to be on its best form. The city successfully cleared the land, built the new infrastructure as planned, and had things looking very posh for the Expo. In all, 246 countries and 50 organizations participated; 56 country pavilions were on display, where people from around the world dressed in costumes that they don't really wear anymore and did dances they don't really do, as they polished up those antiquated stereotypes of culture that are no longer applicable in the world we live in. The big show was a great success: over the course of the Expo's six-month run time over 70 million visitors showed up, a record turnout.

The theme of the Shanghai World Expo was 'Better city, better life', and was focused on urbanization and environmental issues, introducing numerous new ideas and strategies from around the world. Though what was actually created was anything but.

After all the crowds had departed, Shanghai was left with a fresh swathe of land twice the size of Monaco to redevelop. Of the fifty-six country pavilions – which were mostly full-scale buildings – only four were slated to remain. The rest were demolished and cleared away. To walk though parts the World Expo site in 2014 is to feel you're in a ghost town. In the words of Dutch architect Harry den Hartog, 'it is still a big empty wound in the city'. There is a blip of activity near what was once the China pavilion, now the largest art museum in Asia – a despotic-looking dark red inverted pyramid structure – then nothing much other than empty lots, abandoned structures and construction sites. Going to the Expo museum means walking for twenty minutes through a desolate, post-urban landscape. The waterfront, which was supposed to have been turned into a pedestrian corridor leading to Shanghai's famous Bund waterfront, was deserted when I visited, except for a team of construction workers snoozing on a pile of bricks.

However, big plans are under way for the former Expo site. The event itself provided the means for the Shanghai government to reclaim a huge tract of prime real estate in one contiguous swoop – which can now be sold to the highest bidder and redeveloped. The area is one of the four key development zones in the city's current five-year plan, and a US$483 million initiative is in the works to turn it into an expansive mixed-use district, which will contain luxury hotels, upper-class dining, shopping and entertainment, and of course a new central business district – Shanghai's third. An array of office towers and apartment blocks are already under construction, and the former Expo's axis is being turned into an open-air shopping mall. 'This is going to be a high-end destination. It is going to be a new iconic image for Shanghai', said Pierluca Maffey, a project manager for Atlanta-based John Portman & Associates, one of the firms of architects working on the site (Mirviss 2012). Shanghai is clearly making good on its promise to create a 'better city, better life' – but the question is, for whom?

Who owns the land?

'All the land belongs to the government. The government has the right to clear the land. Take it over, and then to either build stuff on it themselves, sell it to a developer or use it as collateral for loans. They do all three, and they've made a killing doing it', notes Anne Stevenson-Yang in a succinct summary of Chinese property law (Schmitz 2013). The definition of private property in China contributes to the lack of power and legal recourse available to those who have their property requisitioned. There was no semblance of private property from the time the Communist Party took power in 1949 until 1978. Rural land was owned by collectives; urban property was owned by the state. Then, as housing reform picked up through the late 1980s and 1990s, a form of leasing was initiated. While the government would still essentially own the land, usage rights would be granted to companies and individuals for certain amounts of time. Following a long string of reforms, peasants were able secure the rural land that they farm for easily extendable 30-year blocks of time, while in cities residential property could be leased for 70 years, commercial property for 50 years, and industrial land for 40 years.

When people in China buy a house they essentially take over their share of the lease on the land from the developer. So, if an apartment building is built two years after the developer leases the land, those who move in right away will have rights to the land for 68 more years; if a development is 15 years old, the maximum amount of time a resident will have in the building will be 55 years; and so on. House prices therefore fluctuate based on the time remaining on the lease.

Although the Chinese technically own the houses they buy, they do not own the land they sit on. Of course, owning a house without the land beneath it is rather moot, a point that has not been lost on the people of China. Needless to say, the Chinese population is not particularly enamoured of the country's property laws. 'We can't own anything', Da Xia, a young women from Jiangsu province, exclaimed with disgust. She paused before adding, 'Well, I can own my notebook', and then tossed it down upon the table in front of us as though it wasn't worth the privilege. 'Some people spend all the money they've ever made on their home and they don't even really own it.'

What will happen when these leases expire is still a big question. A 2007 law says that in the case of residential property the owner will have the option to renew the lease, pending government approval, although a new transfer of land-use rights contract would need to be signed and, of course, another land-use transfer fee paid. As of now, it is unclear how much people will be charged to remain in possession of their own property. As no residential leases are set to expire before 2060, this remains a problem on the horizon. There has so far been only one batch of cases where property leases have expired, and that was in Shenzhen, the place where this leasing system was first experimented with in the early 1980s. Twenty-year leases were given out then, which began expiring in 2002. When this happened a surprised group of business owners in the now prosperous Luohu district were informed that they would have to pay 35 per cent of the value of the property for a forty-year lease extension or face losing their rights to the land with relatively little compensation.

Nevertheless few homeowners in China are worrying much about the issue yet, especially as the projected lifespan of their homes is so short anyway. A user, xiaobao1757, of the Chinese news portal Netease summed up the issue: 'I've never worried about [what happens after] seventy years; what I worry about is how many years before my home collapses. To tell the truth, of the commercial real estate being built these days how much will still be standing seventy years later?' This is not an uncommon sentiment.

Building a new country, literally

In the past two decades China has systematically levelled and rebuilt a huge percentage of its housing stock. Some 129 million homes have been constructed across the country since 1995; 40 per cent of all homes were built after 2000. Each year 2,000 sq km of floor space, nearly enough to cover Hong Kong twice, is being created in China. However, according to Gavekal Dragonomics, a Hong Kong-based financial research firm, this is still not enough: if China is to meet its urbanization goals it will need to have produced between 40 and 50 million more homes by 2020.

It's not just old buildings in old cities that are meeting their end in China's construction boom. According to the Ministry of Housing and Urban–Rural Development, almost all buildings constructed before 1999 – more than half the buildings currently standing – will be demolished and rebuilt in the next twenty years. Shoddy construction is one of the main reasons for this, as buildings that where constructed between 1949 and 1999 are generally considered to be of low quality, as most were thrown up fast and cheap as housing for work units. Gavekal Dragonomics estimates that between 2005 and 2010 China demolished 16 per cent of its total housing stock, totalling 1.85 billion square metres, enough to completely blanket the Comoros Islands.

Qiu Baoxing, the vice minister of the Housing and Urban–Rural Development Ministry, proclaimed that the average building in China will only last between twenty-five and thirty years before needing to be torn down. While this estimation has been contested, there are few people who assume that the apartment blocks that are going up with lightning speed today will be standing in half a century. For a sense of scale, on average houses in Britain last for 132 years and those in the USA for 74 years.

Li Dexiang of Tsinghua University told the *China Daily* that 'what we see nowadays is the blind demolition of relatively new buildings, some of which have only been standing for less than 10 years' (Yanfang 2010). Modern Chinese buildings are essentially disposable: they stand for one, two or three decades and are then requisitioned and demolished, whereupon bigger, better and more expensive buildings will go up in their place. This fits in well with the country's broader economic structure: houses that can last a century are not nearly as profitable as ones that can be demolished, rebuilt and sold three times over within this span of time. As 40 per cent of construction land in China is created every year by the demolition of older buildings, the financial incentives for these urban upgrades is evident. Demolition, too, increases GDP. Under this strategy there is no limit on development, as once all the available construction land is used it will be high time to start tearing down what was just built to build it again. The Chinese have applied the economic stimulus of consumer culture to urbanization; these shiny new cities that are going up across the country today are like new refrigerators which are designed to break down after a few years of use so you have to go out and buy a new one – built-in obsolescence in urban planning.

What we see in many of China's new cities right now is literally disposable. When a developer purchases a plot of land they are not permitted to sit on it, leaving it barren and unused. China has laws which require the purchasers of development land to build something – more or less anything – within a short span of time after taking possession. In new urban areas where there isn't yet much of a population or commercial presence, developers are often hesitant to invest a large amount of money into constructing buildings that clearly won't make a profit. Instead, they opt to build in waves. The first property they will put up in such a place will often be a sort of dummy round. They will throw up something quick and cheap, then wait until the city comes to life around it before demolishing it and then constructing what they actually intend to make a profit from. Parking lots are a popular choice for developers to build during this interim period; it's a common sight to see massive empty spans of tarmac in the hearts of what are otherwise budding new cities. As leases that developers take out for development land are for fifty or seventy years, depending on whether it's commercial or residential, they essentially have two goes at constructing something that will provide a return on their investment. In a very real sense, what we are seeing now in China's new cities are essentially rough drafts of what will eventually exist.

Out with the old, in with the new; out with the new, in with the newer

For a civilization that is 4,000 years old there is a conspicuous lack of any signs of antiquity throughout China. Outside of refurbished and romanticized tourist areas, China has been nearly sanitized of ancient relics. Even Chinese cities that have been inhabited continuously for over 2,000 years often only provide brief glimpses of their age with an estranged pagoda or a temple gate that, for whatever reason, wasn't smashed to bits and carted away with everything else. China has undergone so many facelifts since the start of its economic boom period that it is virtually impossible to recognize the country for what it once was.

'I don't know this place anymore', said an elderly doctor from Taizhou, a small city in the Yangtze River Delta. His hometown was bulldozed and a new one built from the ruins in barely a decade. He doesn't go out of his home much anymore; the place where he'd spent his life has become foreign terrain. For eighty years he lived near an ancient canal in a small traditional town that was a melange of grey brick, one-storey houses with tile roofs aligned along narrow, winding alleyways. This is all gone now. An array of new luxury high-rises have taken the place of what was once his home.

China's ancient cities are now staging grounds for sparkling new shopping malls, bright neon lights, luxury housing complexes, KTV lounges, and large boulevards packed with expensive cars. The traditional, artistically decorated houses with intricately carved wooden latticework and ornate tile roofs have been replaced with rows of monotonous architectural cubes; winding, narrow residential streets full of character and life have been upgraded to wide, straight boulevards that come together in neat grids; buildings that once hugged the street, creating a lively public sphere, have now been set back dozens of metres from the roadside and tucked behind towering gates. The modern Chinese city looks as if it were formed by stamping the landscape with a giant ice cube tray, leaving evenly spaced, almost identical block-shaped buildings in its wake. Most have become what architects call 'generic cities', places – like American strip malls – that lack stand-out features or architectural character that makes them uniquely recognizable.

Since the early 1980s China has been at war with its own architecture. Even cities renowned for their beauty and antiquity have been 'generic-ified', leaving behind only reconstructed tourist zones and dilapidated *hutongs* that the local authorities haven't yet got around to demolishing. In some cities, like Hangzhou and

Taizhou, genuinely historic neighbourhoods have been evacuated and demolished, and anachronistic replicas put up in their place – rebranded as tourist sites.

Taizhou replica old town

An old neighbourhood in Jiangsu, Taizhou is having its centenary this year. To commemorate the anniversary it is being demolished. It is being bulldozed, carted away in dump trucks, and its residents relocated to apartment complexes somewhere just outside the limits of the developed city. This is the usual procedure in China for anything older than a handful of decades. Though what is surreal here is that neither a shopping mall, nor an apartment complex, nor a government building is going up in its place. No, Taizhou is tearing down an old neighbourhood to rebuild a virtual replica of it. Upon the ruins of what was once a traditional district made up of narrow, meandering alleyways and century-old grey brick houses is going up a modern district of narrow, meandering alleyways and brand new grey brick shops and restaurants. The upgraded version of this district has been dubbed Hu Jintao, after the former Chinese president, who is said to have grown up there.

When I first set foot in Jiangsu Taizhou in March of 2012 this neighbourhood was just starting to be redeveloped. There were still people living in it, and the demolition and construction crews were just starting to move in. I would walk through this community and chat with the typically elderly residents who were clinging to the homes they spent their lives in for as long as they could before being taken away by the tide of progress. Most of the other residents had already been whisked away to brand-new apartments in another part of the city. But the grip of the geriatric stragglers was slipping fast – the bulldozers were closing in.

It is in the old communities like this where China's old traditions continue to live on, but this is a way of life that's being sledge-hammered into oblivion. It was in this neighbourhood that I sat in on a practice session of a group of traditional musicians. It was here that I observed Buddhist funeral rites being performed in a home. It was here that I have regularly been intrigued by an almost endless array of antique machines, tools and implements still being used as they have been for centuries.

I met an old man under awkward circumstances during one of my walks here a year ago. Every other house surrounding his had already been demolished; the ruinous piles rose around his home as high as its rooftop. His quaint, small house stood as a beacon of calm and order in a sea of destruction. I walked into his courtyard. Vines twisted over the alley leading to his doorway and laundry was hanging from his windows. I peered through those windows at a home that was still functioning as though it wasn't in the middle of a debris field.

At the height of my trespass I turned around to find that the old man had sneaked up behind me. He was peering at me curiously, but he waved his hand in a friendly way. His facial expression hinted at amusement and surprise rather than offence or territoriality. I offered a greeting and told him that I admired his home. He smiled and treated me as a guest. He was going to remain in his home for as long as he could. I was looking at a new kind of homesteader: rather than going out into the wilds and building an outpost of civilization, he was making a stand in a place that everyone was being forced to leave.

'Nobody wants to live in a place like that', remarked a woman who ran a nearby café, once I had returned to the developed portion of the city. 'Not even that dog wants to live there', she said in scorn as she pointed to a pampered poodle sitting at a café table with its owner.

I had just asked her if there was a possibility that the people who were living in this old neighbourhood didn't want to leave. She laughed heartily at my sentimentality: of course they want to leave; the old homes are not fit for habitation and they have been

given nice new ones by the government. This is the propaganda
of relocation. The public is told that the evicted are provided
for adequately, and those who stay put are whiners grubbing
for more money. Sometimes this is the case, but all too often
nothing could be further from the truth.

Relocation in China is an incredibly complex issue. I came
to China with the mindset that relocation is inherently negative,
but that is not always the way it is. Sometimes the government
coming into an area and seizing property is akin to a get-rich-
quick, 'moving on up' scheme for the people who live there, as
they are compensated very well. However, this practice is also
often shrouded in corruption, empty promises and dictatorial
actions; it is equally likely that the evacuees will have their property taken from them for a pittance and they be moved to a poor
location. So the ethics of relocation in China does not neatly fit a
single model; each case must be evaluated on its merits.

Something the café owner said stuck with me: the old homes
in this old neighbourhood were run-down beyond repair. The
demolition crews that I watched at work were simply expediting
a process that was already at an advanced stage. These houses
were a hundred years old, and they looked it. To put it simply,
the people living in these places did not seem to be winning
the battle against natural decay, and many of their homes were
falling down of their own accord. When I first began coming to
this neighbourhood prior to the demolition initiative, I observed
that the walls of many buildings were severely bowed, the
stucco was chipping off in large chunks, and many of the bricks
beneath were crumbling. The roofs of many of these houses
were bowed, and some had already caved in. These places were
at risk of being flattened by the force of gravity alone. Some
homes had already descended into ruins; tall grass was already
growing up between their disjointed sections and fragments as
they lay in heaps upon the ground. The entire neighbourhood
was degenerating before a sledgehammer struck a single brick.

To be clear, these were not the proud and solid *hutongs* that cover districts of Beijing; they were the meandering alleyways of a geriatric ghetto that the modern era had more or less forgotten about – up until recently when the city decided to knock it all down and start over.

The redeveloped version of this old neighbourhood will have solid brick walls, nicely carved wooden trimmings, indoor plumbing and modern amenities, but it will have none of the essence and life of the original. And buildings are not all that is being demolished as these old neighbourhoods are torn down. The way of life, the community and the way that people interact with each other also change when street-level communities are replaced with apartment complexes. The community ethos in China's traditional communities is thick: everybody seems always to be in the streets, sitting out on benches in front of their homes, talking to each other. Although it is being rebuilt to look similar, the new neighbourhood will be for a completely different purpose. Rather than being a place where people live, it will be an area where people shop and dine. It is to be a knock-off of itself, a mock-up of the Old China, whereas just a year ago it was the real thing. 'It is like tearing up an invaluable painting and replacing it with a cheap print', Tong Mingkang, deputy director of China's State Administration of Cultural Heritage, said about architectural replication projects such as this.

A year later I returned to see how this neighbourhood was faring and to see if I could find any of the residents that I'd previously talked with. I found the old man whom I had surprised on my prior visit. He was still there, but his house wasn't. He was sitting on a chair before a mound of rubble that was once his little home, staring blankly off into the distance at a world long gone.

Clearing the land

Land is cleared systematically in China, but public input is not part of the system. The people who live within the path of development are evicted whether they want to be or not and relocated to places that are not of their choosing. While some end up better off for the move, many millions of others claim otherwise.

Abuse of power, corruption and the misappropriation of funds ripple through China's urbanization movement. Governmental authorities in cahoots with developers regularly sell land from under rural collectives and entire neighbourhoods in existing cities to make a profit, which all too often doesn't trickle down to the people who are losing their homes, land and livelihoods. A much-noted example is Wukan, in Guangdong province, whose villagers say the local chief had been selling off hundreds of hectares of the collective's property for over thirty years, kicking farmers out of their homes, leaving them without land and work, all without compensation. This incident came to a head in September 2011 in what came to be called 'The Siege of Wukan'.

After organizing and petitioning the national government twice without receiving a response, the residents of Wukan began protesting the land seizures publicly, eventually attacking the local government office, a police station and an industrial park. As part of the mediation process, the villagers were given the right to select thirteen delegates to negotiate with the government on the issue. When five of them were abducted by security forces, which resulted in one being beaten to death, the villagers rose up and ran the Communist Party and police out of town. A siege then occurred where a thousand riot police encircled the village, preventing any food or supplies from getting in. Eventually, the provincial government stepped in and allowed the villagers to vote for their own officials democratically by secret ballot. This was the first election of its kind in the history of Communist rule in China. The first election was held in March 2012: Lin Zulian, the leader of the protests, was elected to the position of village chief.

This incident was eventually dubbed the 'Wukan Spring', and a pro-democracy murmur could be heard resonating through the country. Could this spread? Could it be the start of a broader democracy mobilization? The answer was an unequivocal No. Finding himself and the rest of the democratically elected village government politically and economically hamstrung, unable to make real change or reacquire the misappropriated land, Lin Zulian voluntarily relinquished his position as village chief. His replacement faced the same challenge: how do we fund this village? Where is the money going to come from without selling land? The Wukan Spring ended up being a democratic dead end.

What was unique about the Wukan incident was the outcome, not the cause. Forced evictions and demolitions have become epidemic in China. In an ongoing survey, which had been conducted five times since 1999 through a partnership between the Landesa Rural Development Institute, Renmin University and Michigan State University, it was found that 43 per cent of the villages across China had land taken from them within the past decade and upwards of 4 million rural Chinese were being relocated each year. Of the relocated, only 20 per cent received an urban *hukou* (household registration that allows access to public services like schools and health care), scarcely 14 per cent were provided with social security, less than 10 percent received health insurance, and just over 20 per cent were provided with schooling for their children. Another investigation by Tsinghua University found that more than 64 million families, roughly 16 per cent of the total population, had their homes demolished and/or land requisitioned since the beginning of China's economic boom period. Some 20 per cent of these property seizures were reported to have been uncompensated, leaving 13 million families without a home, land or, all too often, the means to acquire a fresh start somewhere else.

Large-scale demolitions and relocations are happening through every province and in almost every city of China. This isn't something that's restricted to the rapidly growing eastern cities or the boom towns of the interior; it's everywhere. Shanghai as well as Sanya is being refaced, Guangzhou as well as Guiyang is being expanded, Beijing as well as Baotou is eating up its rural suburbs. The mayor of Taiyuan, the capital of Shanxi province, earned the nickname 'Point the finger' Geng, because it's said that wherever he points his finger someone's house is demolished. Even far-flung Hailar, a small nowhere city in the extreme north of Inner Mongolia, is surrounded by rolling seas of new high-rises and has its own horizon of cranes. More often than not, where there's a story of construction in China there's a story of eviction.

This is so ubiquitous that stories like these hardly even qualify as news:

Houses Demolished without Warning in Beijing
Two houses in Bagou village in the Haidian District of Beijing were destroyed by bulldozers on 22 October without advance notice to residents. An official warned the remaining residents that their houses will be demolished by 26 November 2013.

Over 200 people including from Haidian District law enforcement, Haidian District Court and public security officials participated in the demolition at Bagou village on 22 October. Some of them were wearing bullet-proof vests and helmets and some were carrying handguns.

At 9 a.m., the demolition team cordoned off the village and began to demolish houses. The court officials said that they were 'implement[ing] the decision of the Haidian District Court to demolish illegal housing'. Two of the remaining six houses have been torn down. The homeowners, He Fengting and Zhao Xiuming, who tried to protect their homes from the demolition, were barred from entering their houses. They witnessed their homes being torn down by a bulldozer. Totally unprepared for the sudden demolition, they could not take any personal belongings with them and are now homeless. (Amnesty International)

Violent Forced Demolition in Nanchang, with Residents Holding Gas Tanks and Threatening to Jump off the Building

March 28, in Jiangxi province Nanchang City, at the intersection between Beijing East Road and Shanghai North Road, a confrontation happened between the forced demolition crew and city residents, during which a man confronted forced demolition crew sitting on window sill with a compressed gas cylinder in his arms, and a female house owner clashed with forced demolition crew on the rooftop, threatening to jump off after being surrounded.… The forced demolition crew charged up to the rooftops, driving off all the residents, and seized all the gas tanks and the national flags hung up by the homeowners. Because they were outmatched in force, some of the homeowners could only powerlessly and helplessly look on as the bulldozers downstairs demolished their houses. (Netease, translation by ChinaSmack)

In most cases, the Chinese media won't cover stories about forced demolitions unless there is a major public disturbance or someone is killed. 'There's so much demolition. If all the demolitions were reported, maybe there wouldn't be enough space in all the newspapers, television and radio stations in China', said Yan Lianke, a well-known Chinese author who recently had his home demolished in Beijing.

Forced eviction and property requisition without adequate cause and fair compensation are technically illegal in China. The country even ratified the International Covenant on Economic,

Social and Cultural Rights, which says 'the Committee observed that all persons should possess a degree of security of tenure which guarantees legal protection against forced eviction, harassment and other threats.' By decree of the Chinese constitution and property law, areas zoned as urban can only be requisitioned for initiatives that support the public interest, though what 'public interest' is remains undefined. As a general rule, when the Chinese government uses terms like 'public' or 'the people' what it really means is 'the Chinese government'.

Forcing so many people out of their homes and off their land is generating waves of discontent over the country. Recent official figures state that 20,000 people throughout China file formal complaints each day with the various levels of government; 80 per cent of these have to do with issues resulting from forced eviction and property requisition. It has also been estimated that 65 per cent of the 180,000 mass social disruptions that occur throughout the country each year are sparked by land and property disputes. It is clear that the physical refacing of China is cutting some very deep social scars, especially as these numerous protests and appeals more often than not go without adequate reconciliation.

As China's urbanization push breaches the rural frontier more and more, large swathes of farmland are being re-zoned as urban and the peasants who once lived there are losing their claims to the land in exchange for an urban *hukou* and a modern apartment. According to Tianjin University, China had 3.7 million villages in 2000, but ten years later that number had dropped to 2.6 million. In a single decade, China lost over a million villages – nearly 300 per day – as the country spirals down towards the agricultural 'red line' of 120 million hectares of arable land that must be left available for farming, the only real limit to urbanization.

Taizhou eviction

'Beijing has lots of preserved buildings, why can't Taizhou?' Mrs Zhang asked as we stood on the rooftop patio of her home. It was a moot point in her case, as her house now stands alone as an isolated island of Old China in a sea of rubble. The ancient neighbourhood of meandering alleyways and age-old grey brick homes that covered this area for hundreds of years had already been demolished, cleared away, effectively erased from the slate of modern China. Now there was only one reminder that this historic neighbourhood ever existed at all, and that was the house I was standing in. The building itself was a mixed-era agglomeration, having an old, 100+ year-old grey brick section connected to a more modern, very well kept three-storey house that was the family's main living quarters. It, too, is on the chopping block of progress, and is set to be demolished – as soon as Mrs Zhang and her family can be removed.

In the year Taizhou was founded ancient Egypt's Ptolemy XII Auletes was born, the Scythians were preparing to conquer Parthia, and Buddhist monks were just beginning to carve meditation caves in the sides of stone plateaus in the Deccan. This small city, which was originally known as Haiyang, first arose in the Han dynasty, when the Chinese developed paper, started making blast furnaces to manufacture copper, and invented acupuncture, the sun dial, glazed pottery, the wheelbarrow, tofu and the hot air balloon. This perennially minor city existed through the rise and fall of the Roman, Zapotec, Maya, Byzantine, Holy Roman and Mongolian empires. The city survived through the Six Dynasties period, the Sui, Tang, Song, Yuan, Ming and Qing dynasties, the Republic of China, the Japanese occupation, Mao, and the current economic boom period. For 2,100 years Taizhou has sat on the banks of the lower Yangtze River, but in the past decade city officials have seemingly been at war with this long history, and have set out to remove all indications of it.

The Zhang family, who can trace their lineage in Taizhou back 300 years, have been living in their property for more than a century. Eight people spanning four generations live in the house; the oldest being 90 years old, the youngest just 9. Red banners are now draped over the house with slogans such as 'We are common people, we are not officials' and 'A violation of the law' printed upon them in bright yellow letters, and 'Where is the justice?' spray-painted upon the outer wall of the courtyard. As the last remaining 'nail house' refusing eviction in this area, the Zhangs go about their days in the middle of a construction zone. Around the house is a large dirt field that has already been cleared, flattened and prepared for construction. Backhoes and bulldozers are busy at work, foundations are being dug, and men in hard hats holding clipboards and walkie-talkies are barking orders.

The developer has a surveillance team monitoring the Zhang house day and night, watching for any sign of it being vacated so the demolition crew can be called in. I looked out at one of these men standing in front of a small corrugated steel shack by the entrance gate of the construction zone; his gaze was focused on me, he was smoking a cigarette, talking on his phone. 'We have not left the house in three months', Mrs Zhang told me, 'because if we do they will destroy it. We have someone bring food in to us.'

Mrs Zhang had reason to worry: all of her neighbours have already been cleared out of their homes and dispersed to apartments or hotels. She told me how eviction squads took the houses one by one. 'Like thieves they did not wear their uniforms when they took the people away and destroyed their homes', Mrs Zhang explained angrily as she showed me pictures and videos on her mobile phone of her neighbours being evicted.

The refacing of Taizhou and the impending demolition of the Zhang home is in no way unique or out of the ordinary in China. Such actions are so common that it has become a common jest in Chinese social media to use the term *chai na*, which means 'in the process of demolishing', as the transliteration of the English name for their country.

The family told me they tried to seek legal recourse to prevent the demolition, but got nowhere. 'The courts belong to the government and the government wants to destroy the house', Mrs Zhang explained.

'A long time ago we used to fear the Japanese, now we fear our houses being destroyed', said Mrs Zhang's elderly mother-in-law.

Mrs Zhang showed me the paperwork that informed them of the impending demolishing, as well as the offer of RMB2.2 million (US$322,000) for her 800-square-metre home. The Zhangs said that they had no interest in the compensation, stating that it was too low, but that it wouldn't matter anyway even if it wasn't. 'My family has lived here for generations. We don't want the money, we don't want our house destroyed, we just want to live here.'

As I looked around their home it was clear that the Zhangs were startlingly unprepared for people facing a forced eviction that could strike without notice. Their porcelain plates and vases were still on display in old wooden cupboards, the family deities stood proudly on their ornate alter, traditional-style landscape paintings were still hanging on the walls, stone carvings were still on display, and all their potted plants, furniture, pet turtles and fish were all arranged as if they would be there for good. The family intended to go down with their ship.

'We will protect our home with our lives', Mrs Zhang declared. 'The law can't protect our house, so we will use our lives.'

Extreme actions to protest forced evictions are not uncommon throughout China. Since 2009 at least fifty-three people have resorted to self-immolation to protest the demolition of their homes. In December 2013, thirteen people from Wuhan drank pesticide in a mass suicide attempt in Tiananmen Square in reaction to being evicted without compensation. In May 2011, a farmer from Fuzhou detonated three bombs in government buildings to protest the seizure of his land. The residents of Zhuguosi, near Chengdu, surround their village each night in a human ring in an attempt to prevent demolition squads from moving in as they sleep.

'In China', Mrs Zhang continued, 'when people don't have a house they have nothing.'

For now the Zhang's ancestral home still sits in the shadow of a towering high-rise complex that sprouts up from the Wanda Plaza shopping mall across the street. The Dalian Wanda Group Corp., which owns the Wanda chain of shopping malls in China and the AMC chain of cinemas in the USA, is headed by Wang Jianlin, the richest man in China. His company has bigger plans for Mrs Zhang's property: to build another thicket of luxury high-rise apartments to complement those already across the street. I asked Mrs Zhang what she would say to Wang Jianlin if given the opportunity. She thought for a moment before responding: 'I would tell him that everybody has their own dream. Not everybody wants to live in an apartment. We don't want to live in a cage.'

'This represents our roots', she said. 'Chinese culture cannot be replaced by money. What a pity to destroy this.'

A week or so later the eviction squad showed up. 'It was around three in the morning. They closed off the street and a hundred police in riot gear charged in', a man who witnessed the event told me. 'The family was on the roof yelling things through a blow horn. They said they didn't want to leave. Something about wanting more money. I heard windows breaking.'

The Zhang family went down with their ship.

This orgy of demolition and construction produces massive amounts of waste. On average, constructing a 10,000 square metre building produces 500 to 600 tons of waste and 7,000 to 12,000 tons when demolished. Construction refuse amounts to 30 to 40 per cent of all waste from China's cities (Yanfeng 2010). In 2011, Wilson W.S. Lu, from the University of Hong Kong, estimated that over 2 billion tons of construction waste was produced across China. Only 5 per cent of this is recycled. For the rest, 'there's no measure to deal with it', according to Lu, and it often ends up stockpiled on the outskirts of cities. A well-known case of this was in Beijing's Chaoyang district, where a mound of construction waste rose into the sky eight storeys high, showering local residents with dust whenever the wind blew. It is also estimated that, for each kilometre of Beijing's Fifth Ring Road, there is half a ton of waste piled up, most of which comes from the city's myriad construction sites.

Land sales

So, given all the social upheavals and political problems, why is so much land being requisitioned in China? The answer, unsurprisingly, is economics: local governments make money selling land – a lot of money. In fact, land sales are one of the main streams of revenue for municipalities. According to the World Bank, local municipalities in China must fend for 80 percent of their expenses while only receiving 40 percent of the country's tax revenue, so the deficit needs to be funded from elsewhere. Selling land and developing new areas currently represent one of the main ways this is being accomplished. This is not just some additional fiscal provisioning either, as a little over 40 per cent of the money made by cities results directly from land sales – and the profits are huge.

According to the Landesa, Renmin University and Michigan State University joint survey, local municipalities can make forty times more money per acre of land than they pay out to the people who once lived on it. In their case studies, the average amount that local governments paid out to the residents of requisitioned rural land was US$17,850 per acre, while the average selling price to developers was US$740,000 per acre. According to China's Ministry of Finance, profits from land sales made US$438 billion for local governments in 2012 alone.

As collectively owned rural land cannot yet be sold directly to developers for commercial, residential or industrial development, the value of it is vastly lower than that of urban construction land, which is fair game for development. This gap in the real-estate value scale presents a prime money-making opportunity for local governments, which just happen to be the only ones with the power to change the designation of land from rural to urban. So local governments buy low at rural prices, re-zone the land as urban, then sell high to developers, pocketing the difference. While the profit margin of municipal land sales is startlingly vast, the proceeds really do generally go towards funding urban necessities, like social services, education, health care and welfare, along with further infrastructural development – corruption aside.

The trend is continuing to grow. In 2000, the proportion of land sales to municipal governments' other revenue was 9.3 per cent; by 2011 it was up to 74.1 per cent. To put it in stark terms, China's current fiscal system forces local governments to depend on land sales, which creates a situation where cities need to keep expanding and developing in order to be able to afford to function. Viewed in this way, China's urbanization movement can be likened to a runaway train.

Manufacturing land

Along with manufacturing new cities China is also manufacturing the land that some of them are built on. Urban construction land is one of the most valuable commodities that a Chinese municipality can have at its disposal, but what happens when it runs out of land to sell? For some cities, the answer is clear: they simply make it themselves.

Like most other municipalities in China, Lanzhou, the capital of western Gansu province with a population of 3.6 million, wanted to expand its central core. The only problem was that the city is on a 50 km strip of land that's wedged in a valley, hemmed in by mountains. Knowing that they were soon going to run out of development land, and have to face the fiscal ramifications, the city's officials decided to try to remove the very obstacles that prevented its growth: the mountains.

The first two attempts at moving mountains were failures. In 1997, the Daqingshan Project aimed to remove a 1,689-metre-high mountain that rose above the city to create a little extra land that could be sold to developers, as well as improve the quality of the city's air, which is extremely polluted due in part to its being hemmed in by the mountains. It was thought that removing the mountain could increase air circulation and whisk away the smog. However, once half of Daqingshan had been removed the project died. The money ran out, and in any case it was discovered that getting rid of the mountain did nothing to improve air quality. Not to be deterred, Lanzhou's officials tried again. This time they began flattening 41 square kilometres of mountain. This project too was soon cancelled, for reasons that have never made it into the public record.

Refusing to give up, Lanzhou decided to try another strategy to
create more development land. Perhaps growing weary of flattening mountains, city officials decided to fill in a river. They packed
a tributary of the Yellow River with earth and then tried to sell it
as construction land. It was only when they had finished that they
realized the soil and subterranean water had become saline. In
order to save its drinking water supply the city had to frantically
dig out the river again and set things back to how they were.

Still Lanzhou wasn't done. In 2012 it returned to mountain
slaying. This scheme, aptly called the 'New Lanzhou Project', was
a provincial government initiative backed by the central government as part of its 'Go West' campaign, which sought to develop
cities on China's western fringes. More than a thousand excavators
at a time were unleashed on 700 mountains in a 25 square kilometre
area so that a massive new district could be built. The cost of the
mountain culling? US$3.65 billion. This seems like a large sum to
spend, but Gansu governor Liu Weiping claims that the projected
GDP for the new district should top US$8 billion as early as 2015,
and officials claim that it could bring in as much as US$45 billion
in yearly output by 2030, when it is set to be completed.

Shiyan, a city in Hubei province with a population of 800,000,
sought a similar solution as Lanzhou for its land deficiency
problem. Originally a village, the place has grown up through
thin mountain ravines in meandering rivulets of urbanization.
In 2010, the city began an ambitious US$2 billion project that
consisted of blasting off the tops of hundreds of mountains in the
hope of increasing its stock of construction land by 70 per cent in
order to lure new factories and housing developers.

Like Lanzhou and Shiyan, the city of Longkou, in Shandong
province, also found its expansion ambitions stunted by natural

barriers. But here, rather than mountains, it was the sea hemming it in. The local government complained that forty-four commercial initiatives worth over US$16 million apiece had been halted due to the limited supply of land. So city officials began looking seaward for their next frontier. In 2010, they began removing 300 million cubic metres of soil and stone from a nearby mountain and dumping it into the bay. A few years and US$3.17 billion later, seven new islands rose above the water's surface, providing an additional 35.2 square kilometres of development land for apartment complexes, resorts, corporate offices, golf courses and industrial parks. By 2020, 200,000 people are expected to live on these new islands, which are projected to yield an annual revenue of US$47.56 billion.

Reclaiming land from the sea is nothing new in China. During the Qing dynasty (1644–1911), it was not uncommon for farmers to undergo large-scale projects to trap sediment in the Pearl River Delta to create more agricultural land. Hong Kong has been reclaiming land since the 1860s; its international airport is built on what was once ocean. Through the 1940s and 1950s China engaged in large-scale land reclamation initiatives for salt production. In the 1960s and 1970s land was reclaimed for agricultural purposes. In the 1980s and 1990s the motive was fish farming. In the current era, land is being created in coastal zones to build housing developments, tourist attractions, ports and industrial areas. Between 1949 and 2000 land was reclaimed from the sea at a pace of roughly 240 sq km per year, but by the 11th Five Year Plan (2006–10) this rate had nearly tripled, as a surface area equal to Singapore was being added on to China annually.

The methods of reclaiming land from the sea are relatively straightforward. There are two main ways: (1) shipping out and dumping massive amounts of soil onto existing islands, thereby expanding their size, and (2) erecting breakwaters around the mouth of a river, and allowing the area within to silt up naturally. The first time I saw the result of land reclamation was in Shanghai's Nanhui New Town, a 133 sq km new development, 45 per cent of which is on newly created land. The new land was claimed by building a massive barrier wall out in Hangzhou Bay, which caught the soil as it went out to sea. As the area silted up the wall was repositioned further and further out until the desired amount of land had been claimed. On the ground, it is almost impossible to tell where the natural coastline ends and the manufactured land begins.

Land reclamation projects have spread down China's entire coastline. Every coastal province currently has large-scale projects under way to extend their terrain further out into the sea. In addition to Nanhui, Shanghai is continuing the construction of the Yangshan Deep Water Port, which is on an archipelago of ever-expanding, artificially produced islands, as well as creating a 6.5 sq km, 80,000-person 'city on the sea' in Hangzhou Bay. Tianjin port, the largest in north China, was constructed on 107 sq km of land that was reclaimed from Bohai Bay, and this is in addition to two additional islands of 45 and 30 sq km that are currently being built nearby. Tangshan built the Caofeidian economic development zone on an area of reclaimed land twice the size of Los Angeles – and it's not done yet, as plans are under way to add on a San Francisco-sized portion by 2020. In Guangdong province, Dongguan pumped US$1.36 billion into reclaiming 44.6 sq km of land, while Shantou is tacking on a new area of 24 sq km. On Hainan Island, the city of Sanya has created something dubbed 'Oriental Dubai' by building an islet for luxury hotels and a port for international cruise ships. In Zhejiang province, Zhoushan has dumped US$14.5 million into the ocean, literally, in exchange for an additional 4.1 sq km of construction land; Yuhuan county manufactured land for a new area the size of Milwaukee; and Taizhou expanded its city another 266.7 sq km – more than twice the size of Paris. Topping every other province, Jiangsu is currently reclaiming twenty-one parcels of land from the Yellow Sea, totalling 1,817 sq km, an area the size of London combined with Munich.

Coastal land reclamation in China has become a developmental free-for-all. Though many of these projects come with huge price tags, the resulting spoils make it worth the investment: filling aquatic areas with earth can produce a hundredfold return on investment (Li 2012).

The value of construction land in China should not be under-estimated. The creating, selling and developing of land is what keeps the country's domestic economy rolling. The story of China's future will be told in what these places become after the land is prepared.

THREE

Of new cities and ghost cities

What is a ghost city?

Throughout history ghost towns have started out as boom towns, and contemporary China without a doubt has more boom towns than any other country has ever had. When discussing China's new urban developments, the term 'ghost city' or 'ghost town' is technically a misnomer. A ghost town is a place that has become economically defunct, a location whose population and business base drops to ineffectual numbers. In other words, it is a place that has died. What China has is the opposite of ghost towns; it has new cities that have yet to come to life – and most of them are still in the process of being built. However, in practical terms, the two types of place have startling similarities, namely the lack of a population and economic pulse. It is for this reason that the term 'ghost city' has been redefined to describe many of China's new developments. According to China's National Science and Technology Department's Terminology Committee, 'A ghost city is a geographical term referring to an abandoned city with depleted resources, a high vacancy rate, few inhabitants, or that is dark at night.' According to the *International Business Times*, 'Ghost cities are the result of prematurely built and underfunded urbanization projects that lose backing midway through completion.'

The general working definition for a ghost city in China is a new development that is running at severe undercapacity, a place with drastically fewer people and businesses than there is available space for.

What is a Chinese city?

Before we can understand how new cities are created, we need to understand what a city in China actually is. In China, the word 'city' is an administrative term alone; much of the land area that falls under the authority of a municipality is urban in name only. In the West, we tend to think of cities as being large masses of urbanization, housing millions of people in high-density conditions, with traffic jams, crowded subways and streets full of people. In China that's not necessarily the case, as the term 'city' simply means that a municipal government presides over a given area.

In practice, the political divvying up of land in China is akin to zoning, of which there are two main spheres: urban and rural. Which side of this line a given span of land falls upon determines what it can be used for and how it can be developed. Land that is zoned as urban falls under the control of a municipality, and is automatically referred to as 'city'. As more and more land is being re-zoned as urban, the geographical reach of China's municipalities grows and grows, which leads to cities that contain hundreds or even thousands of square kilometres of farms, villages, small towns – sometimes even mountains, forests, grasslands and deserts. So, in China you can be way out in what appears to be the countryside while still technically being in a city. Shanghai proper is 7,000 sq km, but over 2,000 sq km of this is cropland. Chongqing is a more extreme example. This municipality, sectioned off from Sichuan province in 1997, has 30 million residents who live in a 'city' the size of North Carolina; yet, according to Demographia (2015), only 7.2 million of them live in a truly urbanized landscape. The provincial city of Chongqing is in fact 99 per cent rural and known for its mountains (Cox 2014). China has cities even larger than this. Jiuquan, in Gansu province, spans 191,342 sq km and stretches for more than 600 km from east to west, while Inner Mongolia's Hulunbuir ranks as the largest municipality in the world at 263,953 sq km, an area that's larger than New Zealand. Nevertheless, most of what these super-large municipal entities contain is empty, undeveloped space. Contrary to their nomenclature, they are definitely not very urban places.

The population counts of Chinese cities are likewise mis-leading, as not everybody who lives in a municipality neces-sarily dwells in an urban landscape. When we learn that an internationally unknown city like Changzhou has a population that's on a par with greater Boston, our first reaction is that China is a very crowded place. But Changzhou, like most other cities across China, is a conglomeration of an urbanized core with villages, counties and industrial zones. Only 800,000 of the city's 4.6 million people actually live in an area that could be described as city-like. This leads to the question, how many of China's 700 million+ urbanites are truly city dwellers? China is urbanizing rapidly, but it is still a very rural country.

The boundaries of most Chinese cities are being pulled out further and further from their central cores, putting more land and people under the administration of municipalities. The scale of these expansions is staggering. In the past fifteen years Shanghai's population has grown by 8 million and its size has increased nearly sevenfold. Even the relatively minor Changzhou recently received approval from the central government to absorb another 1,872 sq km of surrounding farm land, an addition larger than London. As Chinese cities expand, a major discrepancy rises to the surface: the lack of a global standard of what actually constitutes a city makes China's urban areas appear far larger and more densely populated than they actually are. This has led to a lot of confusion in the international media – such as *Time* erroneously naming Chongqing the world's largest city in 2005. More exact English language terminology is needed to delineate the urbanized parts of Chinese cities from the rural. Hence more colloquial, less well-defined terms such as 'urban core' or 'built-up area' are widely used when focusing on the parts of Chinese cities that are actually urban.

These massive and diverse metropolitan areas are a relatively new development in China, as prior to the 1980s the country's cities fitted a more conventional definition, being mostly made up of urbanized cores with only a little farmland on their outskirts. At that time, provinces were divided into prefectures, which were more or less the equivalent of a county in the United States. Each prefecture was divided into cities and counties, the former containing the bulk of the urbanized areas and the latter the rural. Then, after 1980, when China began placing increased importance on its cities, a major shift began to occur and prefectures began to be phased out. The authority of the prefectures was transferred to a city within their realm, which then became known as a prefecture-level city. So suddenly these newly christened prefecture-level cities took control of vast areas of land that contained not only their namesake city, but also other cities, rural counties, towns and villages. This was a major turning point in China's urbanization movement, as cities were given control over vastly larger expanses of land and resources, and by extension a much more prominent role in the administration of the country.

The political structure of Chinese municipalities

Prefecture-level cities are divided into county-level divisions. A county-level division can be a county proper (*xian*), which is traditionally a rural administrative unit, a district (*qu*), which is an urban unit, or a county-level city. However, in the early 1990s, when China's urbanization movement was picking up speed, rural counties (*xian*) began being phased out in favour of urban districts and county-level cities. Within all three of these county-level divisions exist towns, which are sometimes further divided into villages. Taken all together, a single provincial or prefecture-level city in China can contain urban districts, rural counties, county-level cities, smaller cities, towns and villages. This is how China can have cities inside of cities, and villages that are under the authority of a municipality. Translations into English can be confusing: the word 'city' is a little vague, as in this context it can be used to describe a prefecture-level city, a county-level city or a smaller city, even though these are three very different political entities in China.

Depending on their size, most cities in China contain anywhere from two or three to more than a dozen county-level divisions (districts, county-level cities, counties). These areas can contain millions of people on their own, and some were once independent cities that grew into larger urban conglomerations. A good example of this is Wuhan, whose core is a combination of the historic cities of Hankou, Wuchang and Hanyang. The various county-level divisions within cities can very much appear and feel like different places, as many have their own downtown areas, which are often completely separated from other urbanized areas by large industrial and agricultural buffer zones.

Types of new Chinese urban development

Various types of new urban development are currently being constructed across China, the main ones being new cities (*xinshi* or *xincheng*), new districts (*xinqu*), new towns (*xin chengzhen*), and what has been dubbed as 'townification' (*chengzhenhua*). Though, again, what these terms actually mean in practice is a little different from what they imply. Sometimes what is called a new city or a new town is actually a brand new urban development that is built from the ground up; at other times it's just meant as a new administrative division; sometimes it is both. Harry den Hartog, the author of *Shanghai New Towns*, explained this distinction:

> The definition of new town and new city is a matter of translation from Chinese to English... It's different. A new town or a new city in Europe we would call a new neighbourhood or a new suburb. In our definition it's more physical, here it's more administrative. A village or a town or a city, those are administrative units... Gaoqiao is a new town from an administrative point of view, but it's connected with the city of Shanghai ... So that is confusing sometimes.

New districts, also called new areas, are typically massive, county-level administrative zones that have been marked for large-scale urbanization projects or simple added on to an existing municipality.

New cities are just that: new, centralized, 'downtown', urban areas that consist of a commercial core and, oftentimes, a CBD (central business district), which are surrounded by residential areas, schools, hospitals and green space. They are generally large-scale developments that are physically distinct from their surroundings, have their own identity, and are designed on the basis of a holistic concept or macro-plan. New cities can be their own county-level division or a part of a district, and are meant to play a major commercial role in the areas they're built in. They have everything that a city needs to function independently, though they are generally presided over by a larger municipality. China has cities inside of cities.

New towns are smaller scale, centralized areas that tend to have a diminutive commercial area that is surrounded by residential neighbourhoods. They are generally built within districts, counties or county-level cities. They can be seen as suburbs, and are often built on the hinterlands of established cities with a green or industrial buffer between them.

Townification, or *chengzhenhua*, is a marked departure from the conventional way that Chinese cities have developed. Along with the expansion of existing cities and the creation of new ones, which is known as *dushihua* (or urbanization), *chengzhenhua* is the transformation of an existing town or village into a small urban centre. This is done primarily to meet national guidelines that strive to urbanize over 100 million more rural Chinese by 2020. Townification is a lower intensity, much more widespread, form of urbanization, which will define the way China develops economically and socially in the coming decades. Roughly 40 per cent of the 300 million Chinese to become urbanized over the next fifteen years will do so through policies like *chengzhenhua*. Rather than migrating to cities the cities will literally come to them. This is perhaps one of the largest social experiments that has been played out in human history.

Building new cities

A massive exhibition centre stood vacant next to an equally desolate museum, which rose above an unused theatre. Thickets of high-rises touched the sky but sheltered nobody, and a sea of uninhabited buildings stretched out in all directions, seemingly without end. This was the scene in Xinyang's new district. In 2010, a series of satellite images were released by news site *Business Insider*, which claimed that this city in the south of Henan province was an uninhabited ghost city. I entered the district on a smoggy, grey morning in early 2013. I found myself enveloped within a cityscape that had a severe deficiency of inhabitants and an excess of empty buildings, but there was a very good reason for this: the place wasn't built yet.

I was standing in the centre of an entire city that was being built around me. On all sides were the concrete frames of high-rises; men in yellow hard hats and blue overalls were constructing, piece by piece, what will soon be an entirely new urban area. The buzz of creation was everywhere, as a chorus of jackhammers, rivet guns and cement mixers wailed away. As far as I could see down the two main streets were mountains of green mesh wrapped around scaffolding rising up half-finished towers. There was nothing ghostlike about this place. Cars, construction vehicles, and e-bikes clogged the streets; head honchos drove around in black SUVs with tinted windows surveying their creation; workers paraded back and forth; and bored-looking police officers were languidly hanging around on street corners.

I walked over to a colossal housing development that took up the entirety of a super-block that stretched for half a kilometre from intersection to intersection. There was a community of villas on the west side and dozens of high-rises clumped together on the east. This single block was large enough to have been a free-standing urban centre in and of itself. But it wasn't close to being completed yet. Looking at the half-built apartments was like peering through a bare ribcage: you could see right through them. I wondered about the specifics of buying a property in this yet-to-be-inhabited city district, so I walked into the showroom of the compound's sales office. I found two saleswomen and a young man standing in a row, perpetually at attention, behind a counter.

'How many people live here now?' I asked one of the women.

'Nobody lives here yet', she replied, and then added, 'We are not open.'

'When will you be open?'

'Not until 2015.'

'If I bought an apartment, when could I move in?' I asked.

'In 2015, or maybe 2014.'

It was the spring of 2013, which meant that I would need to wait a year or two before I could inhabit my purchase. Far from its being a forgotten ghost city, people were not even allowed to move in here yet. I found that most of the other housing complexes in the district were similarly not ready for residents. This is not uncommon. Most of the new homes that go on the market in China do so long before construction is actually finished, so there is a considerable time-lag between buyers purchasing a place and their being able to move in.

China is transitioning from being a geographically lop-sided country with a few massive, rich cities in the east to being one with major population centres evenly dispersed across the land. Some 300 million more Chinese will become urban in the next two decades, and the plan is for smaller places like Xinyang to grow into larger cities that can absorb the bulk of this migration.

For this to happen the country needs to have massive amounts of infrastructure ready to go: new housing, new schools, new administrative centres, completely new cities. 'China cannot afford to wait to build its new cities', observes Stephen Roach, a professor at Yale and the former chairman of Morgan Stanley Asia. 'Instead, investment and construction must be aligned with the future influx of urban dwellers. The 'ghost city' critique misses this point entirely' (Roach 2012).

Of new cities

Zhengdong New District is already larger than San Francisco, but will soon grow threefold and is set to have a population of more than 5 million people by 2020. What's incredible is that it's not even a city in its own right; it's just one district of Zhengzhou, the enormous capital of Henan province.

I entered Zhengdong via its new high-speed rail station, which is on the far eastern edge of the district. I was dropped into the heart of a massive construction site. Layer upon vertical layer of half-built skyscrapers stretched into the distance before me. I looked at a mock-up of a shopping mall whose outside walls were built but lacked an interior, and walked between uncompleted towers that were still swathed in green mesh and scaffolding.

In 2000, Li Keqiang, now China's premier but then the governor of Henan province, declared that Zhengzhou was not fulfilling its potential as the province's growth driver; it should be, he said, the new economic hub of central China. To this end he initiated a development scheme that would reshape the city. Thus started in 2003 with a US$25.8 billion investment to build Zhengdong New District. After initiating the project, Li quickly rose to become premier, the second highest post in the Communist Party. His speciality, not coincidentally, is urban development; it is often said that he is the architect of China's broader new city movement. This ascension is partially due, no doubt, to his role in Zhengzhou.

With over 11 million people and growing a rate of 9.4 per cent per year, Zhengzhou's population is ever on the verge of meeting its carrying capacity. In the past decade alone the number of people in the city doubled. So the need to expand and modernize was very real. The fact that many of China's historic cities have been rendered obsolete is one of the major drivers behind the current building boom. Rather than fighting long losing battles against gridlocked traffic, urban migration and overburdened sanitation systems, many cities are starting over and building new cities from scratch outside of their historic cores.

These new cities essentially act as modern, better functioning, car-friendly complements of the existing cities. Municipalities all across China are doubling down and building newer versions of themselves. Shanghai has Pudong, Kunming has Chenggong, Tianjin has its Binhai New Area, Changsha has Meixi Lake, Beijing has its new financial district, and Zhengzhou has Zhengdong. James von Klemperer, principal designer of the Meixi Lake Ecocity in Changsha, puts it this way: 'Over the last ten years, China's cities have grown in two ways: by increasing density within the historical cores, and by adding new cities adjacent to the old. The latter phenomenon has resulted in a twin city paradigm.' The old city of Zhengzhou is currently packed bumper to bumper with cars, rendering its curvy and narrow streets a vehicular war zone; its sidewalks are strewn with parked cars and full of manically ridden electric bicycles. The city is a scrambled mess that has been brought to breaking point by a population that has outgrown its bounds. China's new city districts are meant to act as pressure valves to release this build-up.

China's new cities are also often made to be recognized; they are built on an epic scale. And indeed no amount of monumentality was spared in the building of Zhengdong. Its 3.45 sq km CBD was the last great work of Japanese architect Kisho Kurokawa; it is strewn with postmodern landmarks, such as a museum that looks like a clutch of golden Easter eggs, an exhibition centre shaped like a paper fan, a chubby skyscraper modelled on a pagoda, twin towers that have golden lotus petals sprouting from their tops, and eighty-four other skyscrapers arranged in concentric circles around an artificial lake.

Zhengdong New District is divided into six parts: a CBD, a commercial and transportation zone, a big residential area, a university town, a science and two high-tech industrial parks. The new district provides over 3 million square metres of office space, 400,000 housing units, dozens of shopping malls, golf courses, European-style neighbourhoods, and just about anything else China's upper classes could desire.

One common justification for China's building boom is that it will provide new homes for the hundreds of millions of rural migrants coming into the cities. While this is true for some urbanization projects, it's definitely not the case for places near the CBD of Zhengdong. The average price tag for landing an apartment here ranges from hundreds of thousands of dollars to millions. Developments like Zhengdong are full of luxury homes, beautiful boulevards, and high-class attractions such as opera houses and art museums. Clearly, this place wasn't built for working-class rural migrants looking to plant their first roots in a city. However, as nearly 50 per cent of those looking for new apartments in China are existing urbanites wanting to upgrade, a big chunk of the demand for these luxurious homes is real.

New city building is a very class-conscious affair in China, and places like Zhengdong have set the groundwork for parallel migrations. The 'haves' will escape the congestion of the archaic and crowded historic cities and move to the new districts, whereupon the urban working class and rural migrants will flood into the old city and take their place. So a situation has been created where different social classes live in very different urban environments within the same cities. The incredible disparity between China's rich and its poor is magnified by the new city movement.

Of ghost cities

'It's empty by Chinese standards' is a common rebuttal to claims that China's ghost cities are filling up, but this is based on the false impression that everywhere in China is crowded. China is a very big country that contains mountains, deserts and forests; a large majority of its cities, towns and villages have never had very high population densities. To maintain that China's 'standard' for population density is like that in central Shanghai or Beijing is compatible to applying the head count of Manhattan to the entire USA. While China has the densely packed, big metropolises that it is internationally known for, almost every city, including Beijing and Shanghai, also has wide open, uncrowded areas, many of which were built to reduce crowding in the central cores. The extent of these moderately populated suburbs cannot be downplayed, as they encircle virtually every historic downtown area in the country, more and more people are living in them, and they are playing a major role in China's urbanization movement.

Zhengdong

Although Zhengdong is a classic example of the 'city 2.0' urban upgrade movement that has swept China's big cities, it is perhaps best known as an example of something else: a ghost city.

'We discovered that the most populated country on earth is building houses, districts, and cities with no one in them', began a report on *60 Minutes* in March 2013. The news programme's correspondent, Lesley Stahl, ventured out to Zhengdong accompanied by the Hong Kong financial adviser Gillem Tulloch. 'We found what they call a ghost city of new towers with no residents, desolate condos, and vacant subdivisions uninhabited for miles and miles and miles.' As she narrated, video footage showed scenes of tightly packed high-rises sticking up like a bed of nails and stretching far off into the horizon. 'They're building cities, giant cities are being built with people not coming to live here', she continued. And *60 Minutes* was not alone: since 2010 Zhengdong has been called a ghost city by many international media sources. The UK's *Daily Mail* called it 'China's largest ghost city'. Earlier in 2013 *Business Insider* claimed that 'The central business district features a ring of significantly vacant skyscrapers' (Lubin and Badkar 2013).

I entered Zhengdong a few days after the *60 Minutes* report aired, but what I observed was very different. It was not difficult to locate the landmarks that *60 Minutes*, *Business Insider* and other media sources used to declare Zhengdong a ghost city, but on the ground it was difficult to see their angle. There were just too many people, too many cars, too many restaurants, too much action. The place wasn't fully packed but it was in no way deserted. I then walked over to the Orient Center Mall, which is the place Stahl claimed to be 'all make-believe. Non-existent supply for non-existent demand.' I stepped through the doors and strode by the security guards, but as I lifted my camera to take a shot of the fake Starbucks and Nike signs which

optimistically hung above never-inhabited stores, a voice called
out from behind me: 'Where are you going?'

'For a walk', I replied. A twenty-something man in a business
suit appeared from behind me, and it seemed as if I had been
caught. 'Walk with me', I invited him. He obliged.

He told me his name was Zhou. We walked together into
the belly of the empty mall. Fake signs for Western stores lined
both sides of the hallway to demonstrate what this place could
look like if it actually had any businesses in it. KFC, Starbucks,
Zara, Adidas and Nike were all represented. It seems incredible
to think that China is building mock storefronts with the logos
of famous international brands, but this is in fact the usual thing
that new, yet-to-be-inhabited malls in China do. The buildings themselves tend to be built by local governments or their
agents; there is then often an extended interim period before
they are populated with shops and ready to open to the public.
The phony storefronts basically act as showrooms for potential
investors. It probably beats looking into the raw concrete cavities
that would be there otherwise.

We walked through the mall, which had been constructed
three years before but still didn't house a single shop, and
eventually left the area that had been prepared for show. The
walls no longer had white panelling over them, the floor was no
longer tiled, everything was still bare grey concrete. A group
of a dozen men soon overtook us and marched up a stationary
escalator that looked as if had never been switched on. I tagged
along with them up to the second floor, which was even more
bleak and unfinished than the first.

'Are they investors?' I asked.

'No, they are visitors on a business trip', Zhou responded.

Apparently, this vacant mall in Zhengdong is one of the
places visiting business people are taken on tour. This is typical.
The Chinese don't see financial uncertainty and economic
gloom when they look at their abandoned malls and ghost cities;

they see potential. Likewise, they don't try to hide their massive, underpopulated new developments; rather, they flaunt them. New districts and cities are the showpieces of municipalities, and they are in every way treated as such. I asked Zhou if he thought this mall would ever have stores and shoppers. He responded with certainty that it would be filled within the year. 'More and more people are coming', he claimed.

What the international media have dubbed ghost cities are often really just new cities at various stages of being developed. The abandoned mall that *60 Minutes* filmed in was not an example of 'non-existent supply for non-existent demand'; it was a commercial centre at the mid-point of development.

I exited the ghost mall and then made for another mall that appeared a little different. The Mid Town Seven mall spans eight blocks across the entire southern arch of Zhengdong's CBD. It is completely full of shops, restaurants, and people. This mall was conveniently left out of the international media's ghost city reports. I went into a restaurant and ordered some food. I loaded up the *60 Minutes* story on my laptop and invited the waitresses over to watch. I pushed play and then roughly translated what was being said on the video. The girls watched as a couple of foreigners stood in the very city they work in – the very place we were currently sitting in – and proclaimed that it was deserted. This was news to them.

'But we are here!' one of the girls exclaimed. The others looked perplexed.

'Are they lying?' I asked them.

'Yes, we live here', another girl chimed in.

In his book *China's Urban Billion*, Tom Miller explains the discrepancy between the reports of Zhengdong in the international media and the situation on the ground by pointing out that 'When the satellite photographs of this new district were taken, it was hardly surprising that the public buildings looked empty: many of them had yet to open. In the summer of 2011,

Zhengdong remained a work in progress, yet residential areas that had opened four or five years beforehand were filled with cars and people. Most brand-new apartment blocks were empty, but older neighbourhoods were thriving' (Miller 2012: 128).

By the time Stahl and Tulloch arrived, Zhengdong's GDP was rising by 13.2 per cent per year, and had generated US$1.22 billion in tax revenue the year before. Fifteen major banks, including HSBC, had their regional headquarters there, which processed 70 per cent of deposits and 60 per cent of all loans in Henan province. On top of this, Zhengdong was home to fifteen universities, which brought in 240,000 students and teachers. The place that *60 Minutes* claimed to be uninhabited 'for miles and miles and miles' actually had 2.5 million residents. Stahl and Tulloch did not find a ghost city in Zhengzhou; they created one.

In the year since the *60 Minutes* report aired Zhengdong continued gaining momentum. Zhengzhou's first metro line went into operation and was extended out to its CBD in December 2013. Zhengdong district has also added other business and industrial zones, including the airport economic zone where Foxconn's notorious 300,000-worker 'Apple City' is located. Eventually, Zhengzhou will be connected with neighbouring Kaifeng, creating a megacity of 20 million people that will become the economic heartland of central China. This really isn't the picture that *60 Minutes* painted.

Why so many empty apartments?

The international media have readily reported that China's State Grid once claimed that 65 million electricity meters were not being used; this was interpreted to mean that China had 65 million empty homes. This was a big leap to an unfounded conclusion, as there are myriad reasons why these meters may not have been recording energy usage – such as the fact that a huge portion of these homes were not fully constructed or were otherwise uninhabitable. Since then, other agencies have crunched the numbers a little more carefully and come up with a more accurate indication of how many liveable homes are currently vacant across China. Credit Suisse, using the data garnered by Shanghai University, has claimed that the urban vacancy rate in China is 22 per cent, or around 49 million homes. According to the calculations of the Bank of America's Ting Lu, China has roughly 20 million rightfully vacant homes, after mitigating for those that are not fully constructed and adjusting for the time that it takes buyers to fit them out and move in. Given concerns about the social impacts of the ever growing numbers of empty apartments in their city, the Beijing Police conducted a survey of them in 2012. They found that 3.8 million out of 13.2 million total residences, or 28.9 per cent, were unpeopled. The actual number of deserted domiciles in China is open to debate, but one thing is certain: the world's most populated country without a doubt has the world's largest number of empty homes. Whether the number of dwellings without residents is 20 million or 49 million, the scale of the situation is incredible, and as such is enough to warrant the suggestion that China may be looking at a severe housing oversupply crisis. Nevertheless, as we've already found with so many of the other extreme aspects of China's urbanization movement, there is more to the story.

Residents-in-waiting

New apartment complexes in China are essentially construction sites for years after they appear to be built. The casual observer cannot just look at a new apartment complex from the outside, declare it vacant, and present that analysis as an indicator of China's blundering property market. There is a lot more going on inside those vacant apartments than their exteriors tell.

Some 80 per cent of new apartments sold in China are contracted a year or two before their construction is actually complete. So when we see those stock photos of row upon row of empty apartments illustrating articles about China's ghost cities, it has to be kept in mind that many of them are not actually ready to be inhabited yet – as I found out at first hand when enquiring about buying a new home in Xinyang. Although to an outside observer the high-rises may look ready to go, if one actually walks into them one often finds that many essentials – from connecting utilities to paving streets – still need to be done.

There is also a peculiar twist in the Chinese property market that makes the process of inhabiting a new home take much longer than it does in most other countries. When someone buys a new property in China what they often receive is an empty concrete cavity in the side of a building. Such apartments are called *maopeifang*, which means 'blank house', as they come without any interior fit-out. It is the purchaser's responsibility to hire contractors to turn their vacant hole into a home – to add windows and walls, to install plumbing, bathrooms, kitchens, and so on. This takes money and time. It is not possible to move into or rent out one of these apartments right away, which adds further to the time-lag in the populating of new cities and districts – especially when the first wave of new properties to go on the market are often snapped up by speculators, who make a living in the buying and selling of such slabs of blank space.

Beyond this, many new cities and urban developments often sit virtually empty for an extended period of time even after they are fully built and ready to be inhabited. Many people will purchase property along a city's new urban frontier but most will not move in until infrastructure like shopping malls, supermarkets, restaurants, hospitals, schools and public transportation links are built and in operation. This takes time, and very often future residents don't mind waiting.

One disconcerting fact remains concerning China's empty homes. If the owner doesn't want to live in a property, why not rent it out to someone who does? This would seem to be a logical recourse in most countries of the world, but in China it's something that is more or less out of the question. Although the cost of housing is incredibly high, rental yield is strikingly low at 1–1.5 per cent. Thus the amount of money a landlord can make renting out an apartment for a year is hardly even a hundredth of the property's initial cost. So what's the point of making a few hundred dollars per month on an apartment that costs many hundreds of thousands of dollars – paying for the interior to be fitted out and then dealing with the hassle of being a landlord ever after? 'The problem is when you buy a place you first have to invest before you can actually have someone rent the apartment', one of the designers of Nanhui told me. 'You won't do that ... because the rents are extremely low there. There is no payback. Even after fifty years you won't get payback. Only if you can sell it again do you earn. It's a very, very bad system.' In addition to this, fitting out the interior of an apartment immediately lowers its market value. In sum, what there is to be gained from renting out new apartments often just isn't worth the hassle, so the horizons of China's cities remain expanses of desolation.

Changzhou

Changzhou was named one of twelve ghost cities in China by the *China Youth Daily*, which is a rather unbecoming label for a city that has a 2,500-year history, a population that's roughly equal to that of greater Boston, and is predicted by the McKinsey Institute to be the 57th most economically dynamic city in the world by 2025. Changzhou sits right between Shanghai and Nanjing. Together with Kunshan, Jiangyin, Suzhou, Wuxi and Zhenjiang, it is a part of the emerging Yangtze River Delta megacity that will eventually be home to more than 60 million people. In no way is Changzhou, which spans 4,385 sq km and is still growing, a ghost city. What the reports refer to is the Wujin district in the south of the metropolis, which has undergone a complete transformation in recent years, sprouting hundreds of brand-new high-rise apartments, many of which are currently devoid of residents.

I met James, a supply chain manager for an American farm machinery company, in a café in this district. As is customary among Chinese who are used to dealing with foreigners he only gave his English name. He was around 40 years of age; his polo shirt and jacket were clearly plucked from a mannequin at some high-end, overpriced men's fashion store; his shoes were well polished. There was a MacBook on the table in front of him. James showed up in Wujin around three years ago, around the same time as everything else there. Before this, the district was a construction site. When I mentioned that both the Chinese and the international media had been calling Wujin a ghost city he recoiled in disbelief. 'That's not true', he exclaimed, 'you can come here and see that it's not a ghost city'; he then pointed to the bright lights of the shopping mall that were visible outside the window of the café. 'Wuyi Road is a main road of Changzhou!' he proclaimed with an exasperated laugh, seemingly unable to understand how anyone could see this place otherwise. 'Just look out there: does that look like a ghost city to you?'

On 22 July 2013, exactly two months before I sat in Chang-zhou talking to James, a reporter from *Global Times*, a Chinese tabloid, claimed to have visited this stretch of Wuyi Road in the Wujin district and declared it a ghost city. 'Only one thing is missing, people', he wrote (Dong 2013). His story then described a stagnant new district straining for business and residents, which epitomized the pernicious side of China's building boom. What I found there was something different.

It's actually extremely difficult to cross the street in Wujin, which doesn't sit comfortably with the argument that it's a ghost town. Wujin district is full of cars, the sidewalks are dotted with pedestrians, the streets are lined with shops, the malls are full of shoppers, the cafés are packed with customers until late into the night. Almost every shop on the Wuyi strip that wasn't still being built had a functioning business in it. There is a Golden Eagle department store, a Decathlon, a Starbucks and a Tesco – everything you'd expect in a new Chinese city. There is a rapid transit bus line that cuts through the centre of the development, which allows residents to travel between the new district and the historic city centre cheaply (16 cents). Beyond the rapid transit system, there is also an elevated ring road that cut through the heart of Wujin, tying the place in with the rest of the city. Changzhou will start constructing its first metro line in 2014, which will mainly run directly under Wuyi Road, right through the centre of the 'ghost city'. To put it simply, the place is inhabited.

The ghost city claims were made on the basis that there are a lot of empty apartments here. As I discovered in Xinyang, just because an apartment complex appears empty isn't necessarily an indication that the development is faltering; just looking at vacant apartment complexes isn't enough to tell their story. There is an extended interim period between when the exteriors of residential buildings are built and the moment when residents are able to occupy them. Wujin district is still very much a construction site: a large number of new buildings are continuously going up and many new residential towers are not even ready to be inhabited yet. Going around counting dark windows at night or apartments without air-conditioning units is not in itself an adequate criterion for declaring a place a ghost city.

A much better way to gauge the vitality of a new district is to calculate the population density by land area, survey the number of people in the streets, cars on the roads, the occupancy rate of shops, the success rate of businesses, the number of employees working in the area, and in general assess how lively the place really is. When walking the streets in a new town in China that is truly in the ghost city phase all you hear are your footsteps and the wind; there are no honking horns or women crying out selling fried tofu. The ghost city label is, of course, relative to perception; nevertheless, when walking out of a brightly lit shopping mall within a mass of people who are running through a gauntlet of traffic, it's difficult to understand how anyone could call such a place deserted.

Wujin is a real-estate speculator's playground. In 2012 alone, 62,093 residences, totalling 6.58 million square metres of floor space, were sold in Changzhou – many in the new Wujin area. They churn out apartments fast in China, but not fast enough: the demand is still greater. Whether or not people move into all of these new residences seems to be a mere secondary concern, as the fact of the matter is that they sell, they are traded, they are kinetic economic entities. And this is why: 'The cost of housing rose from RMB2,000 per square metre to RMB7–8,000', James observed. 'At first many people only bought one house for themselves but now they wish they had bought more than one', he said with a hearty laugh. 'By the time you hear about places like these it is already old news', he sighed, 'but there are people who are always smelling for them. They know exactly where to buy.'

Wujin was built as a high-population-density urban district; such places can function economically at a respectable capacity

while significantly vacant. Although most of the new high-rise
towers in this district are not even close to being full, the shops
at their feet are full of businesses, and the shopping mall is
booming in the same way as any other trendy new shopping
centre in a more developed city. Wujin district is a forest of
thirty-storey-plus apartment towers. There are hundreds of them
crammed into an area of around a dozen blocks. If they were all
filled to capacity the place would be extremely crowded. To put
it simply, a city district of partially occupied high-rise towers
still tends to have a lot of people. Housing vacancy rates alone
are a faulty criterion by which to designate places ghost towns.

Economics on the frontier

I met up with a team of real-estate consultants from Colliers on
the eastern edge of Nanhui, a new city that was being built 60 km
from the core of Shanghai on the shores of the East China Sea. I
squeezed into the back of the taxi they'd hired and rode with them
as they checked out a few sites for their client. I asked them about
their work. 'We're like coaches', one of them said. They visit the
plots of land that developers purchase and advise them on what
they should build.

Marco Zhou headed the team, and sat up front next to the
driver. He was born in China but educated in England, was
around 32 years old, wore stylish sunglasses, had a neatly cropped
moustache and beard. By his own admission, he was an East/West
cultural hybrid. Educated, wealthy, young and rising, he was the
embodiment of the new cities he scouted out.

As we drove through the outskirts of Nanhui I asked Zhou
what he thought of the place. 'It has potential', he replied as
he looked out across an expanse of empty fields. His response

was perfect: potential is exactly what is being bought and sold here. Never mind that the place was just a vacant city centre and a hundred square kilometres of golden wetlands. When Zhou looked across this barren expanse it was clear that he was seeing gold of a different kind. I asked him why anyone would be interested in investing in a place that sat so far beyond the outskirts of central Shanghai. 'You have to get in early', he said, and then paused for effect as he looked across the fields. 'Nobody knows what is going to happen here', he added almost mystically. Each new urban centre in China has the potential to boom; the sooner you get in, the more money you can make, or so the thinking goes.

One of the properties Zhou was inspecting was an artificial island floating at the edge of the central lake. He thought his client should build a hotel on it. I almost scoffed and asked him why he thought anyone would come to a hotel way out here in a ghost city. 'Don't worry, man', he replied, 'all that will change.'

Zhou's sentiment seemed to be common among developers here. The day before two plots of development land sold for record prices. Zhou said they went for three times the price he had predicted. A 4,537.8-square-metre lot was auctioned off for US$24 million, a 445.45 per cent premium over the initial offering, while a nearby plot sold for US$37.8 million, a 427.4 per cent premium. These sales sent ripples through the Shanghai real-estate market, prompting Xue Jianxiong, the director of CRIC, a Chinese property sales analysis firm, to state that 'laymen' had contributed to the 'irrational' prosperity of the Shanghai property market. Yet rationality is not a highly prized quality in a feeding frenzy.

I asked Zhou why he thought the plots sold for such high prices. 'Bubble', he responded, and then paused for a moment before continuing. 'It's all one massive bubble, and it will explode.'

I asked him what he thought would happen if his prediction came to pass. 'Don't worry, man', he replied with a flippant laugh, 'the government will take care of it. The government will lose a lot of money but we will be fine.'

Zhou spoke with absolute assurance and demonstrated the prevailing attitude of investors in China's new cities. They all talk about the bubble that's soon to burst, while they inflate it even further. They assume that when it pops their government will be there to pick up the pieces – and given the track record of the Communist Party in such matters there is little reason to doubt this. When new cities start to sink in the market economy the central government steps in to keep them afloat.

We were now slowly driving past the main built-up area of Nanhui, where unfinished towers rose, virgin shopping malls sprawled and uninhabited office blocks sat empty. The consultants told the taxi driver to slow down so they could take in the view. They began oohing and ahhing. The big vacant buildings impressed them. The lone female member of the team let out a squeal when she saw the new, though completely vacant, high-tech park. Where I saw desolate buildings they saw the raw potential for profit.

'What do you think of all these abandoned buildings?' I asked Zhou as we continued the tour.

He just laughed. 'It is just a matter of time', he said. 'They will all be filled. It's just a matter of when the government is willing to give the right price. I give it five or six years; by then this place will be filled.'

This kind of sheer optimism epitomizes the typical reaction in China to new cities. Nobody is giving up on them, few people are worried, and for many the game has just begun.

Suddenly Zhou asked, 'Is this different from how you build new cities in America?'

I nearly burst out laughing. 'In America, we don't build new cities.'

In China, the building of new cities is a normal, almost everyday part of life. 'China is very busy. So much is happening here. It's like a war zone', Zhou commented as he peered out of the taxi window at the new office towers of Nanhui that were fading in the distance. He repeated: 'The only question here is when.'

FOUR

When construction ends
the building begins

People need to be given a reason to move to a new city which goes beyond it being beautiful, modern and having a good museum. Jobs, industry, entertainment, health and education systems need to be in place and functioning before they will come in large numbers. Everybody knows this, and for every new city built there is a plan for vitalization. For the Chinese, constructing cities is the easy part; making them come to life is a long-term challenge.

To these ends, municipalities in China rarely just build new cities, wash their hands of responsibility and call it a day. Instead, when the main construction phase of a large-scale urban development comes to an end the real building begins. While China can construct what appears to be entire cities remarkably quickly, often within five years, these are usually more or less urban husks rather than places that are inhabitable. New Chinese cities are grown from the centre out, so a central core – which often includes extravagant public squares, commercial and business zones, museums, opera houses, shopping complexes, high-end housing developments and government buildings – will be built first; then more essential infrastructure, such as affordable housing, hospitals, schools and public transportation will gradually be added as the population grows. The process of vitalizing a new city takes vastly more time, energy and resources than simply throwing up some buildings and laying down some roads; a large-scale mobilization is kicked into motion when the backhoes, dump trucks and cranes begin to clear out.

Nevertheless the interim period between when the downtown core of a new city is built and when it is actually inhabitable is a problem that the Chinese government rarely seems worried about. They have the power to move massive numbers of people around the country like armies. China's ghost cities have never been built on the seduction 'if we build it they will come'; rather, the premiss has been 'we're going to build it and make them come' – that is, population by fiat (Miller 2012). Eventually, as local governments lure universities and businesses, and move their offices into new cities, a consumer base is manufactured and the ball starts rolling.

Ordos Kangbashi

They came from Henan, Shanxi, Guangdong, Beijing, and just about every other corner of China to start new lives in a remote outpost in the far west of Inner Mongolia. Ordos Kangbashi was meant to be an oasis in the desert, one of China's new urban utopias that exemplified the country's new-found riches and glory. It hasn't yet worked out that way.

Ordos Kangbashi is a city that shocked the world. It did so not on account of something it had, but because of what it didn't have: people. This is a place that has become known for its windswept, empty streets, abandoned high-rises, elaborate public buildings built for nobody, multiple stadiums without crowds, and roads to nowhere. Kangbashi is a boomtown that went bust before it was even born. That's the story, anyway.

In 2009, Al Jazeera presented Ordos Kangbashi and China's ghost cities to the world for the first time. Its correspondent, Melissa Chan – who later gained infamy for being the first journalist in fifteen years to be expelled from China – claimed to have found the city by mistake while reporting on another story in the area. In her 2009 and 2011 reports, Chan claimed that 'nobody' lived in Kangbashi, and that the place was completely abandoned; she accused the local government of building the city solely to inflate their GDP: 'local officials in the provinces were hell-bent on boosting their regional GDP – often a criteria for their promotion.' And, as we have seen, building a city has the potential to boost GDP growth to unknown heights (Chan 2011). Her stories set the tone for hundreds of others that would follow on media platforms around the world, making China's 'ghost cities' a global phenomenon.

Ordos is often described as China's Texas. Around a decade ago one of the country's largest deposits of coal was found there; this, combined with an abundance of other natural resources, like rare earths and natural gas, saw the city become the quintessential boom town. Ordos soon began topping China's per capita GDP charts, often outranking some Western European countries, such as Spain. As it became rich, the city set out to do what just about every other Chinese city with the financial means started doing at the time: build a new city.

So, in 2003 construction began on a US$161 billion, 355 sq km new district that was intended to eventually house 1 million people. Unlike many new districts in China that are positioned adjacent to or near an existing urban core, Kangbashi was built way out in the desert – 23 km from Ordos's main district of Dongsheng, which is generally referred to as the old city. The initial plan was for the residents of the older, drought-prone Dongsheng to migrate en masse to the new city, which sat wedged between two massive reservoirs and thus had more than enough water. However, the master plan for Kangbashi has yet to come to fruition. Construction was scaled down part-way through: nearly a decade after construction began only 35 sq km and accommodation for 300,000 residents had been developed.

The mass migration from Dongsheng to Kangbashi has also yet to transpire; just 70,000 people moved in. The project soon found itself spiralling into a chasm of debt, falling property values and bankruptcy.

What started out as a new city filled with prime real estate soon felt the forces of the market economy. Property prices plunged from over US$3,000 per square metre to just US$470 by 2011, and many developers went bankrupt. With many of the houses conspicuously dark at night, the city's reputation as one of China's largest ghost cities grew. 'This severe drop, amid declining prices around China, has convinced both the people and developers that Kangbashi is a lost cause', *Business Insider* claimed in 2011. Nevertheless the people who live there haven't given up yet.

I entered the city and saw the infamous Kangbashi landmarks. I gazed upon the museum that looks like a giant golden jellybean, the elaborate opera house, the library built to look like a gigantic row of books, and the immense stone statues of Mongol warriors as well as the 50-foot-tall bucking horses in Genghis Khan Square. These entities have become the ominous pre-emptive icons of the sinking of an Atlantean nation that brashly built too much too quick.

It was all gargantuan; the entire place simply wasn't built to human scale, which is partly due to the fact that Kangbashi has one of the largest public squares on the planet running through the centre of it. To walk around central Kangbashi is to feel as though you are in a ghost city, as there are few people in the streets, and public life simply doesn't exist. When questioned about this obvious fact by the *China Daily*, Chai Jiliang, the city's chief publicity officer, tried to explain it away by saying, 'why do local residents who mostly own private cars and have convenient public transportation have to walk on the streets if there are no major public events?' (Wang 2012). He had a point. You don't walk in Kangbashi; it's a car city, designed for people who want to drive from one place to another. It's far too grandiose to get around any other way.

China's new cities are monuments. They are trophies commemorating the rise of the municipalities that built them, and there is an overt tendency to overdo it. Rather than building comfortable new districts on simple, human-centric plans, they often construct imperial creations that awe the masses and show the power of their creators. These cities are perhaps designed to be viewed from above, as their streets and plazas come together like colourful tapestries, which surely titillate officials and developers on their helicopter fly-overs. When observed in aerial or satellite images, the artistry of Kangbashi is revealed. Far from being a vacant expanse to scurry across, its central plaza is emblazoned with beautiful circular, sun-like gardens and artfully assembled geometric shapes. However, when these aerial views were revealed in the international media, all that was focused on was how empty the place appeared to be.

It takes some time to find the people in Kangbashi. If you walk through the centre of town and saunter around the public buildings you are liable to meet very few people. Cars will occasionally pass by, but that will be it. Yet if you turn down a side street and head a block or so east you will come to the city's main public complexes and fully inhabited streets. At the centre of this area is a massive dining complex, full of restaurants and 400 food stalls, anchored by a McDonald's. It was lunchtime when I arrived and the place was packed with hundreds if not thousands of people. This is where the residents of Kangbashi meet each day, for it's more or less the only place in town to go. The food court was built with a US$16 million investment from the local government. The commercial spaces are provided to the restaurateurs free of charge. Not even McDonald's pays rent, I was told.

I met a 45- or 50-year-old businessman standing in line at a Mongolian sandwich stall.

He told me that he moved to Kangbashi last year from Henan province. I asked him why.

'For business', he replied simply.

'Did most of the people here come from other parts of China?' I asked.

'Yes, except for them', he replied, pointing to the young ladies who were assembling our mutton sandwiches. 'They were here before.'

Kangbashi sits on the ruins of two old ethnic Mongolian villages. When the city was created they were cleared away, their residents moved into apartments. Many of them now run little restaurants in the food court.

After getting my mutton sandwiches I sat down at a table with a couple of young men, one from Shanxi province and the other from relatively nearby Baotou. Both had arrived in Kangbashi the year before; they came for work. 'Last year, nobody was here', one of them told me. 'This year, they come.'

I moved around the dining area, talking with the people who had moved to this far outpost of progress looking for opportunity and fortune. Ye Qiu was originally from Guangzhou. After a summer of work in the USA, she became tired of the big city life, the pollution, and the crowds of the Pearl River Delta. She told me that she came out to Kangbashi for the adventure, the cleaner air, and the better quality of life. She too arrived here the year before. A pattern was emerging: almost everybody I met in Kangbashi had moved there within the past year. Perhaps it is no coincidence that when property prices began decreasing the people began coming.

Ye Qiu told me that she got a job teaching at a school when she first arrived but eventually started up her own tutoring service. 'In Guangzhou you can get a job', she explained, 'but there are a lot of other people behind you waiting for that job.' By going way out to a new city in Inner Mongolia she essentially transformed herself from being a dime a dozen into a linchpin.

She offered to show me around the city. We walked across
a crowded parking lot and got into her car. 'Every family in
Kangbashi has a car', she said with a laugh. 'Some families have
two.' She took me to the Ordos Museum, the jellybean structure
that is the city's main attraction. It had just recently opened.
Entrance was free.

She drove me back through town, pointing out the landmarks. At the southern edge of the city there was an ominous
horizon of half-built high-rises. 'That is where the government
workers from Dongsheng are being moved to', Ye Qiu said. 'The
government is giving them discounts on the houses there.' As
part of the new city's vitalization effort, the government seat of
Ordos is being moved to Kangbashi, and government employees
are being lured into the new district with special deals on
housing. The municipality also relocated a hospital and the
city's top high school into the new district. To further stimulate
the local economy, Ordos provided more than 200 commercial
enterprises with US$3.7 million in subsidies to help keep them
afloat in Kangbashi. The city also offers free bus transportation
and subsidies on gas and other utilities to anybody who moves
in.

Ye Qiu sheepishly admitted that 'At night, a lot of the houses
are dark. We need more jobs and industry.' While Kangbashi
district is running at severe undercapacity, it is in no way
abandoned. Its population density is actually on par with the
USA or Canada.

Ordos Kangbashi is still a work in progress, though just
about everyone I met there seemed incredibly positive about
the place. As I've found with many other underpopulated new
cities throughout China, the residents say they like things the
way they are, and the lack of crowds is one of the perks of living
in such a place. They like the fact that they can drive around
without being stuck in traffic, that they don't need to wait in long
lines at the bank, that they know their neighbours and recognize

the people they see about town. 'It is very small; the people know each other', Ye Qiu said of Kangbashi. 'In Guangzhou, lots of people are around but you don't feel anyone. It's a fast-food city. It is very busy. Here it is very comfortable. There are no long lines, and the people are not strangers.' She paused for a moment, then added, 'I love the phrase "not so many people".'

Yet there is a paradox in Kangbashi. If viewed from one angle the place appears to be on the verge of total collapse. Ordos has racked up US$50 billion of debt (though nearly two-thirds of this was achieved by its other two districts, not Kangbashi) and entire chains of developers and other companies have been falling into default. The city has even been reported to have borrowed money from companies to pay municipal employees, and delayed payments to builders have become a regular occurrence. The place is a prime example of China's 'city supply' problem, where the excessive drive for local governments to generate revenue from land sales and new infrastructure projects has led to the construction of urban areas that extend beyond the bounds of immediate demand.

In the face of this bankruptcy, debt, and plummeting property prices, however, there is still a great deal of money being made in Ordos, which remains a very wealthy city. Even with the plummeting of coal prices, its GDP remains high, topping US$59 billion in 2012, which is US$29,500 per capita – higher than South Korea. In the five years leading up to this, Ordos showed revenue growth of 32.5 per cent, with an annual GDP growth rate as high as 18.5 per cent. This growth and wealth accumulation are happening in a place notable for corporate bankruptcy, debt and plummeting real-estate prices; in a city that has one of the largest 'ghost towns' on the planet.

Breaking the inertia

The first and probably the most pronounced challenge for China's urbanization movement is the catch-22 of new city building: few people are going to move into a city without a commercial base and facilities, and these entities are slow to develop in a place without people. A decent portion of Nanhui New City, on the far outskirts of Shanghai's Pudong district, has already been built. The core downtown went up years ago, half a dozen housing complexes have been completed, and new shopping malls are ready for occupants. Some 50,000 residents have already moved in, and now the fledgling city is starting to build enough momentum to attract a sustainable population and business base. 'It's the hen and egg problem: how do you get people to move there if there are too few facilities, shopping districts, and so on, but how do you move shops there when there are no people?' observed Fanny Hoffmann-Loss, one of the city's designers. She then paused for a moment before adding, 'In China, they have the means to force these things.'

The troops of urbanization

The way China's local governments populate their new cities is simple: they make people move into them. If there is one thing China has a large supply of, it's people, and one of the biggest weapons the government has is that it can control the movements of large numbers of them, shifting the population around the country as a military commander manoeuvres troops on a battlefield. So hundreds of thousands of university students and government employees are essentially turned into troops of urbanization. They are mobilized simply by moving the places they study and work into the new cities and districts that need to be populated. Move the feeding trough and the cattle will follow. This provides China with a mobile consumer base that can be used as the catalyst of commerce in a new city, from which a local economy can sprout. So, where there is a large-scale new urban development in China there will often be new university campuses, new government offices, and a new central business district full of banks and other state-owned businesses.

Universities are usually among the first institutions to be established in a new city, as they instantly plant a large population of consumers where the campuses are created. In Nanhui there are currently eight new university campuses (with three more on the way); these will eventually bring over 100,000 students and faculty into the area. The effect of this migration strategy is evident when you walk down the street: the only people you tend to see are students.

I met a couple of students in front of the city's new, though empty, hi-tech park. They were from Shandong province. I asked them if they liked living in Nanhui. They both grimaced, and one shook his head and said that he did not like it very much. 'What do you do for fun?' I asked. They had no answer. They had been living there for three years and still hadn't found anything to do. They said they studied hard. I could only imagine the surprise they must have felt after travelling across the country to attend university in Shanghai, the world's most populated city, but instead ending up exiled in a scantly populated, partially built new city 60 km away from the megalopolis's centre.

China's system for populating its new cities may be a totalitarian endeavour, but it works. In the 1990s, Dachang township in northern Shanghai was nothing but farms and scattered villages.

When the city set about redeveloping the area, the first thing it did was build a new campus for Shanghai University. When the off-white compound of frill-less, academic-looking buildings were constructed, the students were shipped in. At the start the place was a sterile outpost of progress an hour from the centre of the city by bus. There were no restaurants, no bars, and there was little to do but hang out on campus studying. The scene was not much different there back then than it is in Nanhui today. But in 2013 I found Dachang town a place transformed. Shanghai's Metro line 7 had been extended out to it, making the area quick and easy to get to. There are now busy streets full of restaurants, bars, karaoke parlours, a Walmart, the standard array of fast-food chains, and a big green sign in front of a newly built shop announcing the impending arrival of Starbucks. Students mingled in the streets, cars flew down the wide avenues. New, brightly coloured apartment complexes ring the university campus. The place had been transformed from fields and urban villages into a vital new suburb in just a decade and a half. If I did not know the area's recent history I would have had no idea that it was once a quasi-ghost town populated by nobody other than bored students (see Miller 2013: 130).

Using universities to stimulate new cities is a tactic that's employed all over China. Zhengdong new district now has fifteen universities that bring in more than 240,000 students and staff. In Chenggong, a completely new city south of Kunming, there's an array of new university campuses, including Yunnan University and Yunnan Normal University. In Songjiang, another new district on the outskirts of Shanghai, a 533-hectare university city has been under construction since 2005 that already houses campuses for eight big universities. China's strategy of shipping universities into new cities to artificially create a local economic and population base works. Once a population of students is planted in a new area market forces are set in motion and the momentum is often enough to vitalize the location. Before long a stagnant new area is economically viable and moving beyond the ghost city phase.

In addition to moving in universities, local municipalities also ship in state-owned enterprises (SOEs). Shanghai's central business district (CBD) in Pudong sat stagnant with less than a 30 per cent occupancy rate for years after it was built, but the city's officials didn't worry. They knew they had their finger on a very powerful switch; when the time came they flicked it and forced state-owned banks to move their headquarters across the Huangpu River into the new skyscrapers that were awaiting them. Pudong is now one of the most vibrant and powerful CBDs on the planet, and is the model for new business districts across China. Another example of SOEs being used to start up the economy of a new city is in the new Sino-Singapore Tianjin Ecocity. The place was designated a centre for northern China's animation, audiovisual and publishing industries, and over a thousand businesses, providing registered capital of US$11.6 billion and 4,000 jobs, were moved in, sparking the local economy.

Beyond universities and SOEs, government offices will also be relocated in the new areas. Schools, hospitals, police stations, bus, train and subway stations, maintenance departments, and administration offices are moved in, and along with them come tens of thousands of new workers. It is also a common practice for local governments to provide incentives, such as housing subsidies, for their employees in new cities; once the new centres are fully functional, many move in and establish themselves as residents.

Grinding the gears of speculation

I had previously met Ye Qiu in Ordos Kangbashi. She moved out there to work as a schoolteacher. I was very surprised when she told me that she owned two apartments in Huizhou, in Guangdong province, on the opposite side of the country. She has been living out in Inner Mongolia for three years and only goes back to Guangdong once a year for Spring Festival. She has never lived in either of the two apartments – nobody has. They just sit there empty. This is not atypical in China, a country where large numbers of people own residential property far from where they actually reside. Sometimes these properties are a raw investment, the hope being that property prices will continue rising so they can sell at a profit, or alternatively a way of storing their savings. For others the property is a home they plan to move into some day or give to their children when they marry. In Ye Qiu's case, the plan is to return home at some point, at which time she will occupy one of the apartments; the other was purchased purely as an investment.

I congratulated Ju Li on the purchase of her first home in Xiamen, where she currently lives and works. I then asked her when she was going to move in. She looked at me quizzically.

'We're not going to live in it!' she exclaimed, as though I had proposed something preposterous.

'Why not?'

'Because it is just an investment', she said. 'Maybe we will go to live there when we get old, but I don't know; it's a little small.'

Her new house is located by the airport in a newly developed part of the city, a little far from where she works. So she's just going to leave it sitting out there vacant, yet another of China's 20–49 million empty apartments.

Absentee homeowners spin the wheels of China's new city movement, allowing developers to profit and local governments to continue reeling in money from land sales, though the phenomenon presents a major obstacle when it comes to actually vitalizing new cities and districts. Urbanization is a financial movement: the new cities are being built to serve as catalysts for growth and, ultimately, to make money. But cities are also, by definition, human settlements – which of course need people to function. How can a new city or town become inhabited and thrive when such a huge percentage of the real estate is owned by people with no intention of living in it?

When new cities begin putting properties on the market it often produces a feeding frenzy of market activity. Professional property speculators, layman investors, and people just looking for a place to store their savings pour in and buy up nearly every residential space available. Investment opportunities are scarce for people in China and banks don't really pay interest, so people keep their savings in property. Wealthy Chinese owning a dozen or more homes is not that uncommon. Just about everyone who can accumulate the cash is now buying additional properties as investments; this drives property prices way up beyond what most working- and middle-class Chinese can afford to pay for their first home, which of course they intend to inhabit. It is not uncommon for most of the properties that a developer puts on the market in a new city to be snatched up by investors. A full 80 per cent of the homes in Nanhui, for example, have been purchased by people who merely hope to flip them for a profit. The property speculation market is essentially fuelling ghost cities, as investors are lured in and prospective residents kept out. At present there is no yearly tax on property in China. So owning vacant homes is not a financial drain. This means people can easily buy homes and forget about them, leaving them vacant for a rainy day, for when property values increase enough to warrant a sale, or for when they get around to moving in.

The Chinese government is well aware of how the absentee homeowner phenomenon is impacting its new cities and is taking measures to remedy it. The Shanghai government began cracking down on *maopeifang* housing, and now requires 60 per cent of new apartments that go on the market to be finished and ready for residents to move in. Another strategy to encourage the habitation of new urban developments is to create 'economically affordable houses'. These are essentially homes that are subsidized by the government and sold at 3–5 per cent above the cost of building them to low-income families. This type of home is made for residents, not investors, and there are strict rules concerning occupancy and resale. Currently, affordable housing makes up approximately 3 per cent of China's total stock, but it was announced in March 2014 that the central government intends to boost this to 23 per cent.

However, speculation also plays a fundamental role in the way new cities are populated beyond simply pumping the system with cash. According to the Milken Institute, 'local authorities are especially reluctant to provide land for affordable housing projects because such development attracts low-income residents from surrounding regions and puts ever more pressure on public utilities and existing infrastructure.' The initial wave of speculation allows local governments to vitalize new cities in stages, rather than all at once. If a new area is built and immediately inhabited, then the city would be forced to provide all the facilities that residents need – such as schools, hospitals and public transportation – right away. By allowing for a speculation phase they can add infrastructure slowly as the new area gradually becomes more populated.

Adding to this, urban districts full of high-density housing means that the buildings don't all need to be filled to capacity for the area to function as an urban centre. Even with large swathes of housing unoccupied, the streets of many mature new areas are nevertheless full of people, schools and hospitals are running at capacity, and shops and restaurants are doing business. Shanghai-based architect Harry den Hartog observed that 'in Hongqiao [a western suburb of Shanghai] it's quite high density ... but if half of the houses are maybe empty ... it's still not a dead city, it's still lively.' The Wujin district of Changzhou, which is often called a ghost city because of its high percentage of unoccupied apartments, is so tightly packed with high-density residential towers that if they were all filled to capacity the city would be so jam-packed with traffic and people as to be virtually unliveable. It must be remembered that in China's new cities a lot of space is built in for speculation.

Sustained government involvement

It would generally be thought that if a municipality were to invest the massive amount of money it takes to build a new district, city or town, it would see the project through to the end. But this is not always the case. A new city is often a local government's showpiece, which demonstrates the tact and ability of the officials who have built it, and is sometimes used to enhance the prospects for promotion within the Communist Party. Hence many new cities are rushed into construction, with massive downtown areas built in just a few years. However, when the local officials who built these places move on to another city, their successors are not always enthusiastic about continuing their pet projects. Indeed this is a big issue when it comes to the fate of new cities, given that high-ranking officials in the Communist Party are generally move on from their posts every five years, or even fewer – which is hardly enough time to build an entire new city. As Kellogg Wong, the coauthor of *Vertical Cities*, remarked to me:

> This is as good a place as any to point out a unique situation in China … 2012 was the beginning of a new ten-year cycle of China's top leadership as well as that of the lower branches, where the term is five years, after which promotion or demotion is strictly dependent on performance. Consequently, new officers have little time to implement and execute ideas. Incomplete projects by one's predecessors are simply abandoned, and make or break new ones started.

'Ownership of the project is critical too. The close patronage by local government means that with a change in the leadership of the local government (not uncommon in China), political backing for the project could be suddenly withdrawn, thus jeopardizing the project in the long run' (Piew and Neo 2013).

Wuxi, a city in booming Jiangsu province, is a classic example of how governmental capriciousness can jeopardize the future of a new urban development. The city began building a new CBD during the tenth five-year plan (2001–05) in its Nanchang district, but by the eleventh five-year plan a new local government decided that Binhu district would be the preferable location, so they went ahead and began constructing a second CBD there. Meanwhile, the half-built first CBD sits half-built and lifeless.

I found that many of the towns around Shanghai's suburbs are experiencing a similar fate.

'Anting New City is stuck', a resident of the new German-themed town explained to me.

'This was a project of the old mayor. Now he is in prison.'

'Why is he in prison?'

'Corruption.'

The Birmingham University-educated Chen Liangyu was the visionary and driving force behind Shanghai's 'One City, Nine Towns' suburban renewal project. With him locked up, his development projects have been virtually forgotten, his successors having moved on to new projects of their own. The result is that around the periphery of Shanghai there sits a massive network of new towns suspended perilously between conception and completion.

This story has been replicated across China. It seems that in the case of some large-scale new city developments nobody knows what to do with them anymore. To be clear: sometimes they don't. The development priorities of local governments often vacillate with the revolving chairs of the high-ranking officials. New faces mean new connections, and sometimes the funding that one official had procured for a project is not carried over to his successor – especially when a project has been tainted by corruption. 'In our opinion, the government's long-term commitment to the development of a new CBD is one of the most important deciding factors for its long-term success', remarked Joe Zhou, a researcher for Jones Lang LaSalle in Shanghai. Sustained government involvement is essential if a new urban development is to make it through the ghost city phase.

The metro means everything

The opening of a new metro station is often the ribbon-cutting moment that announces that a new area is open for business.

Metro systems are the sinews that tie China's sprawling metropolises together. Residents tend to conceptualize their cities through their metro network, and a place without a stop is literally off the map. As soon as a new area has a subway stop it is no longer viewed as being external to the city, no matter how far away from the core it actually is. The role that China's metro system plays in the social and economic development of its new towns and cities cannot be underestimated. Many people will buy property in far-flung new towns, but few will actually move in until that tunnel has been dug and the subway begins running. Places without subway access are in the boonies, and nobody in the New China wants to live in the boonies.

The extension of subway networks out to new towns and cities serves a practical role, enabling people to live further from city centres by providing an easy and cheap way for them to commute. One of the biggest advantages of this is that housing tends to be cheaper in the outskirts of cities, so lower-earning urbanites can move out to the suburbs while retaining their jobs in the urban core. A growing problem in China's cities is that centrally located housing has become too expensive for most residents to afford, so a far-reaching subway system can help mitigate the socio-economic imbalance. This outward migration of lower-wage earners gives the city centre access to cheaper labour; workers can find places to live within commuting distance of their work, and new urban developments in the suburbs are populated with residents – providing that there is an adequate supply of affordable housing.

Hence metro systems are often created for socio-economic reasons. It is notable, though, that metro systems throughout China often lose large amounts of money. For example, in 2013 the Beijing subway network carried some 1.74 billion passengers, but at RMB2 (32 cents) per ride it ended up losing US$558 million dollars. China's subway systems live off government subsidies. Beijing alone has eaten up US$3.6 billion in just seven years.

It must be noted that a significant proportion of these losses from running subway networks are due to expansion projects. Beijing, for instance, is more than doubling the size of its system to over 1,000 km by 2020; many other cities are proportion- ally growing their networks too. This means that many of the new towns and districts that are currently hanging off the edge of many Chinese cities will eventually be on the subway map, thereby serving to encourage their inhabitation and vitalization.

The future of ghost cities

Dantu, a new district of Zhenjiang, in Jiangsu province, is prob- ably best known for being one of China's oldest ghost cities. 'The ghost city of Dantu has been mostly empty for over a decade', *Business Insider* reported in 2010 (Rathod and Lubin 2010). However, what I found there in early 2013 was a moderately populated suburb where the majority of the commercial retail spaces had operating businesses in them, most of the apartments appeared to have occupants, and there were people in the streets and in the restaurants. The place wasn't any less inhabited than any other new suburb in the country, even though it took the better part of a decade for this to happen. By guile or by fiat, China does what it can to populate its new cities.

Be that as it may, for the thousands of new developments in smaller, less economically robust cities throughout China, there is a very real question as to whether they will pass through the ghost city phase. Not every stretch of countryside will support an urban ecosystem just because it has been copied and pasted there, and not every expanding city will be able to sustain the new districts it's building for itself. As with any business, there will be failures along the way; China's urbanization push will surely produce its share of white elephants alongside the boom towns.

FIVE

Megacities inside megacities

'Urbanization is not about building big, sprawling cities. We should aim to avoid the typical urban malady where skyscrapers coexist with shanty towns', Li Keqiang proclaimed in his first press conference as China's premier (Ruan 2013). Yet, when you look across the expanses of China's megacities, skyscrapers coexisting with shanty towns is precisely what you find. Urbanization has spread so rampantly and expansively that rural villages and farming areas are literally being surrounded by cities.

The macro-plan of China's urbanization is to spread a multi-tiered network of urban clusters across the country. The system will run on a hub-and-spoke model where megacities, urban conglomerations of more than 10 million people, will be surrounded by smaller cities, which themselves will be the centres of networks of even smaller cities and towns. So when we look at the new map of China we will no longer see large independent cities functioning as singular urban entities but a continuous amalgamation of interconnected urban zones that blanket the country.

The debate over how many megacity clusters China will create is ongoing, but current estimates are that there will be thirty to forty by 2030. But China's network of urbanization doesn't stop there, as some of these megacity hubs will also be linked together into even larger mega-regions. According to Keiichiro

Oizumi of the Center for Pacific Studies, 'mega-regions are not individual cities, but rather economic zones formed through the linkage of multiple major cities.' There are currently three mega-regions extending down the east coast of China. In the north is the Bohai Bay Economic Rim, which could end up being a 260-million-person urban zone that covers Beijing, Tianjin, parts of Hebei province, and all the cities surrounding Bohai Bay. At the belt line of the country is the Yangtze River Delta, where the Shanghai mega-region, with its 80 million population, stretches to Nanjing in the west and Taizhou in the south. Further south is the Pearl River Delta, which is becoming an urban colossus of 42 million people that will contain Shenzhen, Guangzhou, Dongguan, Zhuhai and their surrounding cities. The future of China will be shaped by its mega-regions: megacity clusters inside megacity clusters, spiderwebs inside spiderwebs of urbanization.

What megacities look like

I looked out over a flat, wide-open expanse of farmland, fallow fields and dirt lots stretching far into the distance. A small brick shack was to my right. An old woman wearing a tattered quilted coat, matching trousers and a grey woollen cap was standing outside it. She was bent over a small patch of bok choy, hoeing. Three dogs ran in circles, barking and nipping at each other. A gaggle of ducks scampered down into a small mud pit that passed for an irrigation pond. Chickens pecked at the stones that were strewn over the narrow dirt road. I was in Shanghai, one of the most populous cities on earth.

The images that this city conjures up are of crowds, congestion, traffic, smog, packed subway cars and busy streets. The popular view of Shanghai is the truth: the place is packed, ultra-kinetic and overflowing with humanity. That is true for part of the city. But there is another Shanghai, one more hidden, less well known, and way more empty. It rings the Huangpu central area like a buxom woman hugging a chihuahua; it's a buffer zone full of factories, old villages, broken-down huts, budding new city centres, ghost towns, migrant-worker slums, and enough cropland to cover Los Angeles one and a half times. Shanghai is one of the largest and most rapidly expanding cities on earth, but much of the city is urban in name only.

As noted previously, the term 'city' is an administrative designation in China, not necessarily a description of a particular landscape. So within the boundaries of Chinese 'cities' can be anything from towering CBDs to lowly villages. In modern China you can go from a modern cityscape of skyscrapers, shopping malls and international chain stores to an area of old brick houses and winding alleys, full of working-class people in ragged clothes stir-frying rice and vegetables in the street, just by turning a corner. In Shanghai, this transition is to be found at its most extreme: a fifteen-minute subway ride takes you from China's financial epicentre to archaic farming villages that have seemingly missed the past three decades of economic reform. In one city China's most modern and fashionable rub shoulders with peasants working their vegetable gardens. Li Keqiang may have expressed a wish to avoid the typical urban malady where skyscrapers coexist with shanty towns, but that is exactly what has been created in Shanghai.

Likewise, the outskirts of Shanghai are a scrambled mix of all facets of the city. There is no smoothly expanding sprawl that gradually peters out as it spreads outward. Rather, it's more as if someone randomly flung the seeds of urbanization in all directions towards the city limits and they grew of their own volition. Over time, these seeds developed to become trendy new city centres, strange towns with foreign architecture, universities, shoddily assembled slums, and myriad housing blocks, hemming in countless agricultural areas. 'The farm land that is left over is criss-crossed; it's fragmented now with smaller pieces between infrastructure. There is a kind of gap between the urban areas and what was once countryside', Harry den Hartog, the author of *Shanghai New Towns*, told me. 'Another way to conceptualize these super-cities is to define them as "scape". Scape is neither city nor rural landscape, but a post-urban condition', says Rem Koolhaas, the designer of the new CCTV building in Beijing (Gardels 2014). This is what modern China scholars mean when they flip the old Mao maxim and say, 'The city surrounds the countryside.' In places like Shanghai it literally does.

As China's megacities expand out into rural areas, urban villages fill in the gaps. An urban village, or *chengzhongcun*, is an area that is typically a rural-looking neighbourhood that had previously been swallowed up by the expansion of a large city. Urban villages are China's slums. Although they often do not look nearly as ramshackle as the slums of South America or Africa, and many are relatively well kept, they serve the same purpose: they are the first steps into the cities for the rural poor. Unless you know what you are looking for, these urban villages can often be difficult to detect, as they look no different from any other rural town or village. It's their position within the city that gives them their distinction. 'The *chengzhongcun* ... is a hybrid zone where the urban meets the rural ... where the "centre" meets the "periphery". It is in these hybrid zones that the lives of the urban 'other', that is, the *nongmingong* [migrant workers], are played out and new identities forged and contested', wrote Gary Sigley, a professor at the University of Western Australia. In these areas China's public maintenance and security infrastructure breaks down somewhat. People from all over the country flood into urban villages, most of whom are unregistered, which makes their presence there technically illegal. This, combined with the high rate of poverty, poor infrastructure, lack of social services, and a laissez-faire attitude on the part of municipal authorities, means that these areas often harbour crime and anti-social activity.

These urban villages are often perceived as a threat to a city's modern image. Destroying them is a triple bonus for local officials: they can remove a slum, sell the land, and create a new middle- or luxury-class development in its place.

It is in these liminal zones that the next phase of China's development is being staked out and defined. This is the space where the city proper meets the countryside, where the sprawl meets industrial zones, where luxury suburbs meet camps of poor migrant workers, where shopping malls meet farmland. This is an area that is spiralling in the flux of demolition, building and reconstruction. The next era in China will be about what happens on the peripheries of the big cities. There is no better place from which to view these developments than the outskirts of Shanghai.

The new Shanghai master plan

Beijing may call the shots, but Shanghai is the financial capital of China. Covering just 0.1 per cent of the country's land area, Shanghai supplies 12 per cent of total municipal-derived revenues, and more than a quarter of China's trade passes through its ports.

The city has been growing rapidly: in just fifteen years Shanghai's size has increased nearly sevenfold; its population has grown from 6.61 to over 23 million. Inundated by this torrent of growth the city needed a plan.

The Shanghai Master Plan was revealed in 1999, and set the course for the city to reinvent itself. With the motto of 'One dragon head, four centres', the following twenty-one years (1999-2020) would be set aside to rebuild the entire city. The goal was to position Shanghai as the country's centre of economics, finance, trade and logistics, while re-establishing it as a global hub of commerce worthy of its history. As the city centre continued becoming more crowded, the local government sought to vitalize its suburbs to lower population density and extend the reach of the metropolis. To these ends, Shanghai introduced its '1–9–6–6' plan, which was the blueprint for completely redeveloping the city's suburbs by building a network of new towns, cities and villages. Shanghai would become one large central urban core, surrounded by nine decentralized medium-size new cities of between 300,000 and a million people, sixty towns of between 50,000 and 150,000 people, and 600 villages with roughly 2,000 people in each. These new developments were to be strategically placed outposts of urbanization evenly dispersed around the periphery of the city like spokes radiating from the hub of a wheel.

The new cities and towns were intended to lure away the city's upper- and middle-class residents who were weary of cramped living quarters, traffic jams, crowds and the pollution of the central core with the promise of wide boulevards, open space, trees, lawns, cleaner air, a lower population density and quaint little towns in the suburbs. This was Shanghai's attempt to suburbanize USA-style.

Shanghai is engineering itself to become a 'middle-class utopia'; its new towns colonies of high culture and prestige encroaching upon the city's untamed frontiers. It's not just development that's being shipped out to the periphery, but an entirely new way of life. Included within the 1–9–6–6 plan was the One City, Nine Towns initiative that gave birth to new developments themed on the classical architecture of Germany, Scandinavia, Canada, Italy, the Netherlands, the USA, England, Spain and 'old time' China. Throughout Shanghai's tenth five-year plan (2001–05), most of these 'cultural towns' were built with the vision that they would be suburban utopias that would pull a million of Shanghai's high-resource-consuming, car-driving middle-class and wealthy residents out of the city's core by 2020. As Shanghai was again becoming a global crossroads of commerce and culture, it is perhaps no coincidence that the countries whose architecture was mimicked were precisely those that played a pivotal role during the colonial era. Only this time Shanghai was colonizing itself.

These new towns are tools of cultural influence; they are seeds of modernity that are meant to expand and consume the surrounding landscape, sprouting urban culture in rural soil. Gary Sigley described this movement as being a 'metropole', a term that was originally coined to 'describe the relations between the Western colonial centre and the spaces "outside" which were subject to various forms of colonial power, and of the multifarious ways in which the "periphery" also reflected back upon the "centre".' What is happening in the outskirts of Shanghai is very much a process of colonization.

In the areas where these new towns are located there is a major divide between the local and rural migrant classes and the upper classes for whom the developments are intended. Harry den Hartog explained:

> You see in many of those new towns many informal activities like selling watermelons, vegetables, meat, all kinds of products and also all kinds of services by people of the countryside. They offer themselves, 'I can help you with painting your walls or making a new carpet for your floor or fix the problems in your kitchen or your toilet.' So in general there is a big gap.

With this gap has come an element of conflict. Many of the residents surrounding these 'colonies of civilization' are not exactly pleased with the invasion of Shanghai's moneyed, internationalized set. As Bianca Bosker, the author of *Original Copies*, explained to me at length:

> I found the neighbours living next to China's new Frances and Italys largely displeased by what they saw as a waste of land and money. In the case of Shanghai's Scandinavian-themed Luodian Town, for example, 'locals' saw the European development as out of touch with their needs – its homes too expensive by far – and an unnecessary investment that had replaced a perfectly fine community. To build Luodian Town, its developers first had to evict existing residents from the land they planned to build on, yet the Nordic homes they built have remained mostly empty since its completion. In short, Luodian Town's neighbours have watched a bustling neighbourhood replaced by a ghost town. Others who've seen these expansive theme-towns erected complain that the lavish towns make poor use of good land. Vast villas sit on sprawling lawns that some of its neighbours would have put to use farming even mattress-sized corners of fruits and vegetables.
> These developments also risk exacerbating social tensions in a country with one of the greatest wealth discrepancies in the world. Many of these theme towns are, by design, spectacles of conspicuous consumption, and those who live near them are quick to comment on the lavish lifestyles of the homeowners within. The developments showcase the vast differences between the 'haves' and the 'have nots' in such a clear and drastic way that could make them catalysts of resentment and discontent.

One Fudan University doctoral student in Shanghai exclaimed in disbelief: 'Educated people won't relocate to such a remote area – they'll run right back to Beijing or Shanghai – we don't work as hard as we do only to end up in a cultural backwater!' (Visser 2010). When Chinese developers began building upper-class residential developments in the suburbs of big cities many soon found themselves in an impasse: while the properties generally sold readily and for high prices, few people actually moved in. This has resulted in big cities like Shanghai and Beijing being encircled by upper-class ghost towns. Generally speaking, wealthy Chinese are not going to give up their grade-A addresses in the city centre for quaint, quiet lives in the suburbs – no matter how desirable the towns and houses are out there. What they do instead is live in the city and, when they have a little free time, take trips out to their houses in the outskirts, or alternatively hang on to them for potential resale or perhaps retirement. In consequence, China's suburbanization movement fell flat on its face before it could make any headway. It became clear that the US model of satellite towns surrounding a central city wasn't going to work in China.

China's German ghost city

It was effectively a German town, designed by German architects next to a Volkswagen factory on the outskirts of Shanghai. The place had everything: housing, parks, canal-side promenades, benches, fences, shops, roads, town squares, statues, office blocks, even a church. But it lacked the essential element of a city: a sizeable population. Except for the stray car or motorcycle passing every five minutes or so and an old man pushing a baby in a stroller three blocks away, I was alone as I walked through Anting German Town.

This town sits like a foreign country plopped down in the middle of Shanghai's industrial wasteland. Anting is also often referred to as Shanghai's Automobile City – and this is more or less what it is. There is a VW plant, a slew of car components factories, an F1 race track, slums for Chinese labourers, and a few fledgling attempts at creating modern urbanity for the foreign workers at the factories. Up until very recently this area was a remote industrial zone, but now the world's most populous city is steadily approaching.

I rode on metro line 11 from central Shanghai for over an hour to Anting, 30 km from the city's core. The metro station had opened just a month before, and the next stop down the line was still in the process of being built. A new shopping mall was coordinated to open at the same time as the metro, and within a short span of time this town went from being a remote and difficult-to-access outpost on Shanghai's fringes to having the two main ingredients a new area needs to grow and prosper in China: a modern mall and a subway station.

The German town is only accessible by a single road that discreetly connects to a highway that runs south from Anting's old town. There is a comfortable buffer zone consisting of green space, a golf course, artificial hills and a lake, which keeps the outside world at bay.

The Chinese developers originally wanted a storybook-inspired anachronistic old Germanic hamlet, but the German architects refused: they didn't come all the way to China to construct a joke. Instead, they built a German city like those Germans really live in today: a district full of modern three- to five-storey orange and lime green Bauhaus-inspired buildings equipped with double-glazed windows and central heating. They wouldn't have looked out of place in a trendy new district of Stuttgart or Hamburg. The initial plan was to have Anting German Town cover 5 square kilometres. However, when the construction was only one-fifth completed the project went stale, and eventually fizzled out. Even so, an entire downtown core, with capacity for 50,000 residents, was completed.

In 2006, people began trickling in. But the intake of residents never became a stream – much less a flood that could have pumped life into the place. Although the developers claim that all of the properties sold, only a few were actually ever inhabited. According to official statistics, one in five homes are occupied, meaning the rest stand as empty cavities behind fake Teutonic walls.

I walked around rather aimlessly for the better part of two hours. The buildings were devoid of life, their windows like the empty eye sockets of a skull. I climbed onto a bridge that had collapsed into a pond, which nobody had found any reason to repair. What would be the point? Anting German Town was seemingly built just to fall into ruin. The affliction was straightforward neglect.

I then entered a little square that boasted statues of Johann Wolfgang von Goethe and Friedrich Schiller standing side by side. A voice called out from behind me. I spun around and saw two Chinese men sitting at a cheap patio table drinking beer in front of a bar. I was taken aback: an open business is almost startling in such a barren landscape. I walked over and sat down with them. One introduced himself as the owner of the bar, and his wife stepped outside to join him. I asked why he had come all the way out here to open his business. He looked into the distance, raised his glass to Goethe and Schiller, and said: 'It is very good here; I can drink every day and no one bothers me.' I couldn't disagree with that: ghost cities are good places to be if you want to be alone. But before I could commend him for finding what he was looking for, a trendy looking, 30-something couple walked briskly across the square and took seats at a table. Drinks were soon being passed around as the nine to fivers began drifting in after a day of work.

I then met the other two owners of the bar, and asked why they had started up their business in a new development that lacked the vital ingredients of commerce, namely people. Neither seemed in the least worried that the town was at most only 20 per cent inhabited. I then asked one of their wives if she was nervous about the lack of people. She looked at me with surprise as though I'd just pointed out something she hadn't noticed before. She responded that she wasn't worried at all, and stated that a lot of Germans from the VW plant come regularly. Every Friday night they had a big barbecue and a house band. 'More people started coming last year', the owner's wife explained. When I asked her if she thought this trend would continue, she replied with certainty that it would.

This sentiment was echoed by a translator for the McKinsey Institute. Although her commute is over an hour each way, she said that it's worth it to live beyond the urban fringes of the city. She repeatedly described Anting German Town as wonderful. Not only was she seemingly unworried by the lack of population; she actually revelled in it: 'There are not many people and this is good. My kid can play outside; it is not busy here.' She admitted that the town was more than a little far-flung, and that there was a distinct lack of opportunity and places to work. 'But for me it is good', she said. When I asked her if she thought things would soon change in Anting and there would be more opportunity in the future, she replied disappointedly that she felt there would be. 'But I hope not', she quickly added, 'because then more people will come.'

Another resident backed up the statements of her neighbours, describing Anting German Town as 'very peaceful and lovely'. Her name was Lili; she quit her job in central Shanghai and moved out to the suburbs when her husband relocated his factory nearby. 'It is better for my kids', she stated. 'They can play outside in the streets and there is no traffic and people everywhere. They can ride their scooter, play tennis, golf, and ride their bicycles. It's safe here, not like in the city. We know our neighbours', she continued. 'In Shanghai I never even knew the people who lived right next door. We were always too busy. The people here are so friendly; we are like a big family.' We continued talking about the town; the picture she was painting was very different to that shown in the international media. I pulled out my tablet and opened an article about Anting New Town that appeared in the German publication *Spiegel Online*, and handed it to her.

'Nobody wants to live there' she read aloud from the opening paragraph. 'That's not true!' she exclaimed. 'The plan was for 50,000 people', she continued reading. 'That would be so terrible!' she commented with a cackle. She then explained that she didn't want more people to move in. 'If more people come it will be like the city. Now is enough.' She returned to the article, visibly disgusted. When she finished she remarked, 'That's not the new city I know.' As the article was published in October

2011, I asked if the city has changed much since then. She told me that when she first moved to Anting in 2008 she could walk through town without seeing anybody but security guards and street cleaners. She complained that she now has difficulty finding a place to park. It was becoming clear that these people like their ghost town the way it is.

Shanghai's Dutch ghost town

'This used to be an authentic Asian city with lots of original-style buildings. Now it has been developed and all of that is gone.' Zhou, a home-grown resident of Gaoqiao, spoke as we sat together in the shade of the largest faux church in Shanghai. 'It is a pity', he reflected while shaking his head.

We were in Shanghai's New Netherlands Town, a place that was designed to look just like Holland built in Gaoqiao, a city whose history dates back to the Southern Song Dynasty, although no sign of the area's antiquity is evident anymore. It is now an industrialized zone to the north of Pudong on the east bank of the Huangpu River, which stands just outside the Waigaoqiao Free Trade Zone. It is ringed by tyre and chemical factories.

There is a giant wooden Dutch-style windmill here. There is a canal-side promenade that is almost an exact copy of a stretch of Amersfoort. The Netherlands Maritime Museum, Amsterdam's Bijenkorf department store, and Voorburg's Hofwijck mansion were also duly replicated. The main road through the Dutch neighbourhood is called Holland Culture Street. It is a shaded pedestrian walkway that cuts between four-storey buildings with old-style Dutch-inspired facades. It was obviously meant to be the epicentre of this new town. But there is no shopping to be done here, for most of the shops are closed, and there are hardly any pedestrians. A survey of Holland Culture Street can be completed quickly and easily: there is just a lone restaurant, a convenience store and two or three preschools. All other doors were firmly closed and the windows covered in faux fashion advertisements to hide the empty interiors within. On weekends young couples from central Shanghai come out here to have their picture taken in front of the exotic European-style buildings.

'What do you think of this place looking like Holland?' I asked Zhou as we sat in the shade.

'It is a pity', he repeated. 'Chinese people don't like it, and I think foreign people don't like it either.' He paused for a moment before turning the tables on me: 'What do you think?'

'It is a little fake', I responded.

'Fake! Yes, it is fake!' he roared.

'Do you see anything there?' he continued excitedly. 'There are no bars, no cafés, no places to go. I think when foreigners come to China they want to see Chinese-style cities and Chinese culture.' Zhou then paused for a moment before shifting gears. 'It's not about the buildings', he continued, 'it's about the culture, the people, the traditions. There is none of that here. It is a pity.'

I then asked him why he thought the government wanted it to look Dutch.

'It is said that the Shanghai government wanted to make Gaoqiao a modern city but the local officials here just kept the money. If I was the mayor I would tear all this down and make it an original Asian water town', Zhou ranted. 'If they made it original Asian style and opened bars and cafés people would come. The water towns are nice, people like them. Not like this.' He gestured out toward Holland Culture Street shaking his head.

He had a point: Shanghai's new 'water towns' were way more kinetic than any of its foreign-themed towns. But how could this man really complain? The rest of Gaoqiao was either chemical plants, rust-encrusted industrial ports, sprawl or slums.

'Who would want to live here?' I asked, wondering how developers could ever think they could entice wealthy middle- and upper-class people to move out to this industrial inferno. 'It's all chemical plants, industry and ports, and it smells like burning tyres.'

'Yes', Zhou replied, 'there are lots of factories and it smells like chemicals, like petroleum.' He then thought for a minute and shook his head before admitting, 'Yes, this place is very unhealthy, this place is very bad.'

Nevertheless, Shanghai continues its rapid outward growth, and it looks as if even its toxic industrialized suburbs will soon become prime real estate. Following the media explosion at the end of 2013 concerning Shanghai's free-trade zones, the three main areas in which they are located have exploded in popularity, and the price of property in them has likewise dramatically increased. Apartments were being sold in Gaoqiao for nearly as much as they were going for in downtown Shanghai. Perhaps the officials and developers knew what they were doing.

Thames Town

Thames Town is a 1 square kilometre British-themed new town 30 km from downtown Shanghai that was intended to house 10,000 people in low-density, single-family, European-style villas. Despite the fact that almost all of the properties sold rapidly for insanely high prices (some for upwards of US$3 million) to wealthy investors and property speculators, very few people actually moved in.

I walked into the centre of town and found myself wandering down stone streets between rows of storybook faux-Tudor shops and restaurants. I ended up strolling through the village green, interrupting the photo-shoots of half a dozen brides, and stopped for a rest in front of the Romanesque Gothic-style church that is the town's centrepiece. No services actually take place here; it's basically just a background prop for wedding photos. (In China, couples have professional photos taken, dressed in full wedding regalia, multiple times in the year leading up to their marriage.) All around it was nothing but brides, brides, photographers, brides. None of them knew anything about Thames Town other than the fact that it is pretty, and a good place to have one's photo taken.

I doubled back to the tourist information centre. I walked up to the counter and was welcomed by the three people working there. Then I asked what I believed to be a simple question.

'How many people live here?'

'I don't know', said the man whose job it was to answer such questions.

So I asked the two women flanking him. They said they didn't know either.

'1,000? 10,000?' I asked trying to get some kind of estimate.

'I don't know', the man said again, but this time he was clearly saying 'Stop asking me questions like that.'

I continued asking, but it was in vain: the only definitive information available on Thames Town was that the tourist information office staff didn't know anything about Thames Town. This official position was probably the safe bet. This place has been widely criticized all around the world as a flop, and I definitely wasn't the first curious visitor to stumble in and start asking such questions. I would need to work harder to discover anything.

I walked back out into the street and looked for someone to talk to. Twenty minutes later I was still searching. I couldn't find anybody. The sound of my footsteps was the only thing interrupting the silence. I began to enter the shops, and a striking aspect of the place immediately revealed itself: most of the shops, cafés, stores and restaurants only appeared to be in business. This fact hit me hard when I tried to walk into a café with posters and signs in the windows, chairs on the patio, pictures all over the walls, a fully equipped bar and a decorated interior. There was one thing blocking my way: a gate that was permanently latched shut. It was a fake café, built only as a visual prop, a still life of a business.

I eventually found a café that was meant for actual customers. I was the only one there, which didn't come as a surprise. I ordered a coffee, then asked the woman behind the counter if she was local. She said she was, but she meant that she was local to Songjiang, the broader surrounding city, not Thames Town. I asked her how many people lived in the British-themed experiment. She just shrugged and said, 'Not too many.'

'10,000?' I asked. She burst out laughing. Apparently, this was a bigger joke than I thought.

Thames Town was designed by Atkins, a genuine UK architecture firm, under the direction of Tony Mackay, a genuine British architect. But that's where the authenticity ended. Although there is a statue of Winston Churchill and the buildings look English enough, it's difficult to regard the place as anything other than an anachronistic fantasy – a place that got dressed up, went out to play make-believe, and never came back. The town is somewhere to have your picture taken, not a place to live in.

'It has this almost dreamlike quality of something European', the town's master planner commented to the BBC about the way his work was brought to life. 'It doesn't look quite right', he said. 'It looks false' (Morris 2013).

Of course, you can't expect a newly built replica town to feel authentic, but this place was something else: it wasn't alive. It was like an exhibit at Disneyland, something to look at but not touch. It made you want to walk on tiptoes, and just about the only thing to do was photobomb wedding pictures. There was no history, no story, no soul here, and this inertia seemed to prevent anything else from being created.

The future of Shanghai's new towns

Shanghai's 1–9–6–6 plan was a take on Ebenezer Howard's Garden City design, where a network of small towns separated by green space would be dispersed around a central city. These new towns were meant to be a reaction to the crowded central cores of Shanghai, a way for people to escape and live in a peaceful American-style suburb, but this is not coming to pass. 'The garden cities built around London are remote from the central city; there's a green buffer', Harry den Hartog explained. 'Here [in Shanghai], the distance may be the same but because of development most of the new towns will soon be connected with the original city. So they are not physically independent, they are growing together.' Shanghai's Garden City initiative was intended to beat sprawl, but it has instead become the harbinger of such. When you look out towards the central city from any one of Shanghai's new towns you can see the front lines of the generic city rapidly advancing. The new developments of Shanghai's

One City, Nine Towns programme will eventually become walkable, quaint little neighbourhoods floating in the raging seas of characterless high-rises and overbearing *scape*.

'The train now comes here and there is a shopping mall full of restaurants and a cinema, and a supermarket. All came last year', a resident of Anting German Town told me. Her town is slowly being included within the Shanghai matrix; the encroaching city can be seen looming on the horizon. 'Someday they will build it', she admitted sadly. The same can be said of all of Shanghai's new towns, though this is probably the only way these places will become fully inhabited.

Huaxi

The Yangtze Delta Megacity also contains a place that has dubbed itself the 'world's richest village', which is a good lens through which to view just how extreme China's urbanization movement has become.

I peered through the white billowing emissions that were spewing from the twin smokestacks of a coal-fired power plant and noticed something very much out of place rising in the distance. In the early morning hours of a summer day I looked out across the central Jiangsu plains, and there, amid the typical factories, fields and villages was a skyscraper.

You almost come to expect such surreal scenes after living in China for an extended amount of time, but this skyscraper was something beyond the usual oddity. I was looking at the Zengdi Kongzhong, the fortieth tallest building in the world, the fifteenth largest in China. It is higher than the Eiffel Tower, New York's Chrysler Building, everything in Tokyo, and will top out higher than London's Shard, the tallest building in the EU.

Seventy-four storeys high, it rises 328 metres into the smoggy Jiangsu air. This is the same height as the tallest building in Beijing – which is intentional. Yet there is another reason why the designers chose this height. In Chinese numerology the number 328 is loaded with significance; 32 is associated with business and 8 represents prosperity. This is fitting, as the skyscraper is a massive symbol signifying the economic prowess of a place that has dubbed itself the world's richest village. 'The skies above Huaxi are the skies of the Communist Party. The land of Huaxi is the land of socialism' (Huaxi's village song).

'One village, one man, one miracle', is the popular three-part summary of Huaxi. The village is held up as a model of success for Chinese socialism, a system where every man, woman and child is supposed to get rich from the globalization epidemic, at which point the society will become a communist utopia where all the wealth is shared. While Huaxi may not be exactly what the Communist Party means when it talks about building a 'new socialist countryside', the village's success is lauded nonetheless.

Huaxi was once just a regular agricultural commune. Then in 1969, at the height of the Cultural Revolution, it started up a village-owned textile factory, which was brashly against the rules. Somehow, through political jockeying, grace or luck, Wu Renbao, the village secretary, was able to persuade his superiors to look the other way as the factory began producing and distributing goods. 'I could not sit and watch my people starve to death. We were scared of being poor. And farming alone would never have led us out of poverty', he later said. Wu Renbao practised what the Chinese call 'outward obedience and secret independence', where you show deference towards your superiors but then enact your own policies behind their backs. 'If a policy does not suit our village, I will not implement it', he said. In addition to textiles, the village began producing steel, iron, chemicals and tobacco, which it began exporting abroad under the cloak of political secrecy.

Later on, as China began to enact political reforms which broke up most communes, Huaxi decided to maintain the status quo under Wu's direction. They built more factories and started up more businesses of various types. 'If you just grow crops, you don't really have a very rich life', Wu said. 'You've got to have money. Without money, everything is just empty words.'

Huaxi continued expanding, eventually buying twelve neighbouring villages. The original population of 2,000 peasants grew as workers from other areas began pouring in to work at the village's factories. In 1998, Huaxi became the first commune to be listed on China's stock exchange. Eight big corporations were founded there, and earnings in the range of $3–4 billion dollars began pouring into the village each year.

The streets of Huaxi are flanked with thousands of stone statues of Foo Dogs, lions and other guardians. There is a courtyard with larger-than-lifesize stone carvings of Chairman Mao and his core group of Party heroes sitting in big chairs with red cloth bandannas tied around their necks. Thick rows of trees line both sides of the streets in residential areas, completely surrounding each villa, giving the place the appearance and feel of a campsite. 'We're trying to build an ecological village that looks like a forest garden', Wu once said. All of the houses are identical; from what I could tell, not one had anything on its exterior that marked it as unique. They look uninhabited when viewed from above. To add further to the strangeness, on a nearby hill there are replicas of the Great Wall, the Forbidden City, the Arc de Triomphe, Sydney Opera House, the White House and the Statue of Liberty.

There is only a single row of shops in the village, none of which sells anything special; these include a few clothing stores, a shoe shop, half a dozen low-budget restaurants and a few noodle houses. The retail options here belied a place whose residents were supposed to be incredibly wealthy.

There is a very clearly divided social hierarchy in Huaxi. At the top is Secretary Wu, his immediate family and their relatives. They are followed by the 2,000 original Huaxi residents, who now mostly hold managerial positions in the factories they helped create. They are said to receive a cut of the village's revenue, and all have over US$150,000 in their bank accounts, two brand-new cars, a villa, and free health care. Beneath them are the 35,000 people who live in the twelve villages that Huaxi has recently taken over. At the bottom of the pyramid are as many as 40,000 migrant workers who have flooded into the town in search of work.

The original Huaxi families are said to work seven days a week without any holidays. Some news reports say that the residents are forbidden to even leave the village. Yan Lieshan, a respected Chinese author and journalist, described Huaxi as 'a quasi-slavery system. No weekends. No vacations. No privacy. Everyone listens to one omnipresent and omnipotent god. And a person has to give up much of his freedom in exchange for a relatively well-off standard of living.' Other reports say that if any of the villagers move away they lose all the savings, their stocks, house, car, and all benefits. There are no bars, no tea houses, no cafés, no KTV lounges, no Internet cafés. I did find a dingy pool hall, but it was clearly not the kind of place that any of the rich Huaxi villagers would ever step into. This was by all by design. 'Gambling and drugs are strictly forbidden in the village. There is, in fact, no night life whatsoever … Anyone who engages in speculation will be driven out of the village, and his property confiscated', the *China Daily* reported (Xiao 2003). The *People's Daily* reported that 'Huaxi Village is managed as if it were an army compound.' Wu Renbao publicly defined happiness as having a car, a house, money, a child, and face. 'If you have these five things, you are happy', he said. The residents of Huaxi may indeed have these things, but it seemed as if they had little else. That is, other than their skyscraper.

'This skyscraper will give us the edge', said Wu. 'No other village has one.' Called the Zengdi Kongzhong, it is three towering, shiny blue pillars holding up a giant gold sphere. That it looks like a bowling trophy is perhaps no mistake, as the building truly commemorates victory. Its interior is everywhere plated with gold. There is a golden fountain where golden dragons spit water into the mouths of golden frogs; there is a sculpture of giant golden phoenixes soaring before golden clouds; even the railings and trimmings are plated with gold. On the sixtieth floor there is a golden room that has a US$50 million 1-tonne gold bull at its centre. The village claims that it built the skyscraper to attract tourists, though its prime aspiration is to be a city.

What mega-regions look like

'Ladies and gentlemen, welcome aboard Harmony', a recording rang out over the loudspeaker. 'Harmony' is the literal translation of *Hexie Hao*, which is what the Chinese call their high-speed trains. I couldn't argue with this as I leaned back in a soft seat, stretched out my legs, and got ready to begin a short journey that would take me 165 km from Shanghai to Changzhou in under an hour. Almost silently, the train began rolling away from the platform on the minute of its scheduled departure time, and I was shot down the spine of what is quickly becoming the Yangtze River Delta super-megacity.

The master plan is to connect Shanghai with Nanjing in the west and Taizhou, Zhejiang in the south, tying up all of the sixteen budding cities of the Yangtze River Delta into a singular urban colossus of more than 80 million people. Many of the wealthiest cities in China are accounted for within this urban mass. In terms of per capita GDP, Suzhou, Wuxi and Changzhou routinely top China's richest cities charts; Nanjing and Hangzhou are economic powerhouses; and Shanghai is the undisputed financial capital of the entire country. This is the most economically vibrant area of China; though it covers just 1 per cent of the country's urban area and contains only 6 per cent of its population, it produces 20 per cent of the country's GDP.

The nerve system of this megacity is the high-speed rail lines that run through its centre, connecting the various urban districts into a single, interconnected, pulsating megalopolis. Over 120 pairs of high-speed trains run the line between Shanghai and Nanjing each day, departing every 5–15 minutes. The G class train can cover the 300 km distance between these two cities in a mere hour and a half. To travel the same distance by car takes more than twice as long in good traffic. For scale, the average one-way commute of a Shanghai resident is 47 minutes, and this is without even leaving the city proper. Now residents can easily live in another city along the line and commute to Shanghai for work or vice versa. The speed of these passenger trains along with their frequent departures enables the population of this region to spread out, and seek homes and opportunity throughout the region. For example, someone could live in the lower-cost cities such as Wuxi, Suzhou or Changzhou and commute to Shanghai in the same amount of time it takes for the average Shanghainese to get to work. When a person can wake up in Shanghai, attend a meeting in Nanjing, and be back by lunchtime, these high-speed trains are making the mega-region dream a reality.

The train didn't even get up to top speed before slowing down for its first stop at Kunshan. There was no visible gap between Shanghai's industrial suburbs and this factory town.

Large, cube-like manufacturing plants abutted large cube-like manufacturing plants until the loudspeaker of the train informed me that we were someplace else. It didn't look that way to me, which is apparently a sentiment that officials in Shanghai share. Kunshan is ground zero in the Yangtze River Delta megacity political squabble.

'There are not many people there but there are a lot of factories', a Shanghainese businessman said of Kunshan. 'There are more than two thousand Taiwanese factories just there.' And this is what makes Kunshan worth fighting for. Although, relatively speaking, many industrial parks and manufacturing areas of China lack large populations, they are incredibly valuable to the municipal and provincial governments that preside over them. Selling land to developers is a prime device for local governments to generate revenue, but whether this land is sold for residential or industrial purposes is a very important distinction. Tax is only paid once for residential development land, but industrial land is taxed in accordance with how much is produced on it, meaning it will continuously feed the coffers of local governments. For this reason, industrial zones are prized by municipalities. Shanghai attempted to take control of Kunshan, but was met with big resistance from Jiangsu province, which currently presides over it. Politically speaking, China's mega-regions are mega-debacles. Some of the smaller municipalities that lie within the bounds of the proposed megacities do not want to give up their autonomy and be cannibalized by their larger neighbours, just as provincial authorities do not want to give up any of their prime cities and manufacturing zones to contending tier-one municipalities. In this way, Kunshan has become a symbol of the internal political resistance to China's broader mega-region drive.

For all that, the megacity plan is a way to reduce the runaway competitive edge that China's largest and most famous cities have over smaller ones. As things stand, the growth and status of cities across China is very unbalanced. Beijing, Shanghai, Guangzhou and Shenzhen tend to draw the most investment and the best talent. Companies stationing their headquarters in these cities carry a status and prestige that would simply not be present were they to be based in Jinan, Fuzhou, Taiyuan or Changde. The same can be said for the flow of the most educated and highly skilled workers, who often want to be in key cities where the action is. This creates a race to the bottom for smaller competing cities, who often try to keep up with the big boys by over-building infrastructure they do not really need, lowering the prices of commercial or industrial real estate, and offering bigger subsidies and incentives to attract investment, business, and talent.

The megacity and mega-region plans attempt to mitigate this imbalance and assist underdog cities. By linking together administratively with larger, more economically vibrant urban centres, cities on the periphery can benefit from a sharing of industries. For example, in the Capital Economic Circle decrees have been put under way to relocate 200 companies from Beijing to Tianjin and Hebei province. However, perhaps predictably, this was a contentious gift from the capital as most of the companies that were being handed over were those that consume a large amount of energy or are big polluters. Needless to say, Tianjin and Hebei were not exactly pleased.

Local municipalities' resistance to China's broader mega-region ambitions extend across the board. Many smaller cities tend not to want to give up their autonomy to larger ones in the process of conglomerating; hence these proposed mega-regions are still very much composed of more or less independent administrative units. Irrespective of whether or not China's mega-regions ever become politically seamless entities, the fact is they are being built; physically they are becoming singular metropolitan expanses. The open spaces between Shanghai and Kunshan, Jiangyin, Suzhou, Wuxi, Changzhou, Zhenjiang and Nanjing are being filled in fast: factories, warehouses, colossal high-rise apartment blocks, and shopping malls are rising out of what had been just farmland for thousands of years.

The train soon pulled away from Kunshan and entered into the heart of Jiangsu province. 'This part of the Yangtze River has the most fertile soil and the most economical [*sic*] prospects', I was once told by a representative of China Medical City, a new development just across the river from where I was. Yet, as I looked out the window, it seemed as if the master plan was to asphyxiate as much of this fertile land as possible with a tight seal of concrete in the name of those 'economical prospects'. Small plots of farmland dotted the landscape, but they looked as if they were just waiting to disappear. At regular intervals a cluster of factories, a housing complex, or a small city would pop up, fragmenting this ancient agricultural matrix into a thousand pieces. Farm, factory, warehouse, apartment complex, farm, factory, warehouse, apartment complex ... was how the scenery rolled by at 350 km/ hr. The patchwork of urbanization here still had many pieces missing, but the procession of upside-down L-shaped cranes along the horizon promised that this would not be the case for long. The cities between Shanghai and Nanjing are being connected together through their individual expansion as well as the growth of new districts, cities, towns and housing developments between them. Soon they will be contiguous.

The train didn't have a chance to attain full speed between cities, which to all intents and purposes are in effect already part of the same megalopolis. All of the buildings looked the same; the only way I could tell that I was leaving one city and entering another was that the train sometimes stopped, whereupon a recorded voice through a loudspeaker told me that I was in a new location. Soon enough, that voice informed me that I had arrived: 'Good afternoon, passengers. We have now arrived at Changzhou.' I took one last look out of the window, at the hundreds of high-rise apartments, which looked like a dozen staggered picket fences layered back to back, forming a solid wall of city.

SIX

A new city, a new identity

> With a completely new development you can try to form a new ideal city. Meaning that you also form a kind of ideal society without any history behind it.
>
> Fanny Hoffman-Loss, Nanhui New City architect

China is an engineer's dream. No other country has ever provided urban designers, civil engineers and architects with so many blank canvases upon which to paint their masterpieces. Whereas in most other countries architects will be commissioned to design a single building, a subdivision or at most an entire block, China often grants them the liberty to design entire cities, complete towns, and massive new districts. China has a unique advantage in this regard, as it has the desire, ability and financing to build entirely new urban realms. Obstacles such as evicting tens of thousands of people from their homes, razing entire neighbourhoods and villages, and clearing swathes of development land that extends for hundreds of square kilometres are business-as-usual for the Chinese urbanization machine. This opens up the possibility to create completely new places with all-encompassing, macro-designs that simply couldn't be attempted elsewhere. China's municipalities are also hungry for monumentality, and are often willing to push experimental and conceptually innovative designs that have never been attempted before. In this way, China has become a beacon for the world's architects and engineers, and a renaissance in urban design appears to be on the verge of being born.

Although much of China's experimental urbanism may seem like a lot of flash and dazzle, there is an underlying driver motivated by the fact that the country's existing urban designs simply do not meet the demands of the twenty-first century. Most Chinese cities are essentially row upon row of the same, cube-like buildings that range in height from five to thirty storeys and in colour from off-white to grey – which happens to match the colour of the polluted skies above them. They are crowded places, choked with traffic, and the chaos that results from road rules that are so rarely enforced as to be nonexistent. Cars park on the pavement, forcing people to walk on the road; e-bikes whizz around in swarms, crashing into each other, cars and pedestrians; shops have roaring sound systems that blare out irritating promotional jingles that can be heard blocks away. Everybody seems to be in someone's way, the air makes you gag, and the incessant noise reverberates in your head, crescendoing into a constant, static-like hum.

What is perhaps worse is how identical China's cities now look to each other. Whether one is in Guiyang or Nanning, a redeveloped part of Shanghai or Shenyang, one sees a scene consisting of exactly the same buildings, constructed in the same way, housing the same banks, chain stores and restaurants. Street signs do not help, as for the most part the streets even have the same names in every city. Qiu Baoxing, the former minister of construction, notably observed that urbanization in China 'is like having a thousand cities with the same appearance' (Miller 2012: 133).

The urban monolith that has covered China is a direct consequence of its recent history. When the Communists came to power in 1949 the country was in a shambles. In fifty years

China saw the rapid decline and fall of the Qing dynasty, war-lordism, attempts by the Nationalist government to take control, invasion and occupation by Japan, and a civil war that tore the country apart. Mao essentially won the right to rebuild a land in ruins. This the Communists did using the most expedient and cheapest means possible: they adopted the Soviet model for construction and began rebuilding their cities from the bottom up to be utilitarian and practical. The ethic of mass production was applied to urban renewal: a virtual mould was cast for creating cities, which was then applied across the country. Cities were rebuilt with wide boulevards, buildings became little more than concrete boxes, workers were housed in shoddily built dormitories. This round of redeveloping China's cities was very much government-led, an impersonal approach to urban design, and by direct extension social design, that led to developments that ignored beauty, pleasure and community cohesion in favour of absolute pragmatism. Cities became little more than centres of production or administration, centralized locales where workers produced goods and bureaucracy kept the wheels of the country turning. Due to the dilapidated state of the country in this era, cities needed to be rebuilt fast and cheap. A standard urban design full of standard buildings that would be constructed with standard materials fulfilled this requirement. The movement without doubt successfully accomplished its goals: China was rebuilt very expediently. Significantly, though, much of what was created during this time was more or less temporary: it was not meant to last forever.

At the end of the twentieth century China found itself in a very different economic, social and political environment: new options for its cities had to be considered.

The current model of urbanization is unsustainable

From Guangzhou to Beijing, Shanghai to Chengdu, there is a common and serious problem: the density of traffic. The rapidly rising number of personal cars on the roads of China are clogging the country's highways and jamming its streets, which are more like slow-moving glaciers than fast and efficient arteries of modern transportation. Traffic jams that last for days are not unheard of – one outside Beijing stretched for sixty-two miles and lasted for twelve days. Add to this the notorious air quality that's partly caused by vehicle exhaust, and it becomes clear that China has a traffic crisis. 'They understand that their current urban forms aren't working', architect Peter Calthorpe said in an interview with CNN. 'Consider the long commutes, gridlock and crowded subways. The urban Chinese live in neighbourhoods where build-ings average ten storeys, whereas in America it's two storeys. At such high densities, auto-based cities just don't work.'

Half of the world's new cars are now being sold in China. There are over 240 million vehicles in the country, half of which are personal cars. Beijing alone has over 5 million cars – which is more than the total populations of half the countries in the world. Eighteen cities in China have over 1 million private cars. Even though many large municipal governments are taking measures to curb the number of cars that are allowed on the road, their sales are still growing by 15 million, or 27 per cent each year. Clever residents tend to find loopholes in the restrictions, as architect Kenneth King pointed out: 'We have learned people will always find ways to circumvent any governmental rules especially when it comes to cars. As an example, Beijing tried to restrict the use of cars by allowing only odd or even number licence-plated cars to drive on a given day. To circumvent this rule, many people buy two cars with licence plates one even and one odd number.' The only country in the world that tops China for car ownership is the USA.

However, China's traffic problem is not caused simply by the sheer number of cars. Many of the cities are just not suited to every adult driving their own vehicle. The building of more highways doesn't solve the issue either, as Beijing has discovered. Constructing new highways to cut down on traffic density merely creates the opportunity for more cars to go on the road, and as a consequence the city transport network becomes ever more car-oriented. Not so long ago, 60 per cent of the residents of Beijing commuted to work by bicycle; now it's 16 per cent. Designing new cities to reduce traffic congestion has caused two opposed development strategies to meet head-on. High-density vertical cities, which condense urban environments into smaller areas by building upwards (theoretically reducing the need for cars), and suburbanization, which spreads the population out to reduce crowding, are both being tested as solutions to the traffic problem.

High-density cities are often cited as more ecologically friendly, but in a country like China, with a booming middle and upper class, a city with a high population density means a high density of car ownership. Urban Chinese drive cars not just for convenience but for the status conferred – many people would rather sit for hours in a traffic jam in their own car than take the metro or the bus like some plebeian. So while projects like Changsha's proposed Sky City One, which could cram 100,000 residents into one giant building, are often seen as the future of ecological urban design, in the current context this would mean factoring in tens of thousands of personal cars. While hopeful urbanists attest that nobody living in a sky city would drive a car, it is unclear how this cultural shift would be implemented.

Whereas suburbanizing – thinning out the population by spreading it over a larger expanse of land – does lower population density, it at the same time increases dependence on private cars and requires vastly more land, infrastructure and resources. In the early days of China's new city movement, developing the suburbs was seen as the key to mitigating the population density crisis, and the goal of some municipalities was to spread out their populations like a baker flattens a lump of dough. Cities like Shanghai invested massive resources into building new satellite towns and urban centres around the periphery of their urban core. It looked as though China would try to suburbanize a billion people in the way the USA did with 160 million in the 1950s.

Yet, like most pragmatic plans, it was just too simple. The pitfall of this initiative was that the high-resource-consuming middle and upper classes – those with the cars who were supposed to suburbanize – didn't budge. Another major sign of status in China is a grade-A address. This means the city centre. So, while people bought up most of the properties in the new suburban towns, very few actually moved out to them. That is to say, Shanghai's suburbanization movement just created a network of ghost towns.

Knowing all of this, China's urban designers are now setting out to enact a new strategy of urban design that essentially combines the urban and the suburban, and in consequence experimental cities are going up all through the country. 'What China offers, with its vast market, is a testing ground for the implementation of ideas that a more "experienced"' and hard-nosed economy (such as the one in New York City) would be reluctant to try', remarked architect Kellogg Wong. It is in these testing grounds that the cities of the future are coming to life.

The planned city

Planned cities are going up across China, but they are really nothing new. Since 1136 BCE, when the Duke of Zhou designed the holy city of Chengzhou based on the Holy Field symbol, the Chinese have been clearing out large swathes of land and building entire new cities based on singular plans. They are still at it, though now these planned cities are going up at the edges of almost every city in the country.

The advantage of building planned cities is that an urban area can be constructed as a holistic concept, as a complete organism where each part is intentionally made to complement the whole. Traffic can be well organized, pedestrian areas created, commercial, office and industrial zones optimized, and the living areas idyllically laid out. New ideas can also be tested, experiments can be tried out, and the seeds of a new urbanism can be planted. A major disadvantage is that serious design flaws or bad ideas can be baked into a city, which could be very difficult or impossible to correct later on.

Except for a few choice experimental developments, the typical new Chinese city looks like a spreadsheet when viewed from above. It is a massive rectangle filled with many smaller rectangles laid out in neat horizontal and vertical rows. As Robin Visser describes (Visser 2010):

> It is very common in China that urban planners base layouts of
> vast city areas on regular, rectangular blocks without any reaction

to specific features of the local environment and specific roles of streets in the city structure. The resulting extremely wide, straight, and long roads, subdivided into many separate paths for cars, bicycles and pedestrians, create 'wide rivers of asphalt.' They are very difficult (and sometimes forbidden) to be crossed by foot... It may be seen as the only solution to traffic problems but it does not provide a satisfying urban environment for its citizens and does not offer suitable conditions for many urban functions that include commerce.

These super-blocks, which sometimes stretch for half a kilometre between intersections and can have streets 200 metres wide, have the effect of dividing up an urban area into neat, separated sectors. One side of the street is cut off from the other, and the enormity of the space in between creates an atmosphere of isolation. These are places that are built on almost larger-than-life proportions, which discourages walking and diminishes street life. 'The width and density of streets; the layout of buildings, lots, and sidewalks; and the design of other key features tend to reinforce a move away from walking as a convenient way for getting around, hampering efforts to lower overall carbon emissions', states a World Bank report titled *Sustainable Low-Carbon City Development in China*. 'What's fascinating about these places is that China hasn't opted to copy the latest and greatest in architecture or technology, which it easily could have', Bianca Bosker, the author of *Original Copies*, a book on China's Western-style new towns, told me. 'Instead, it's replicated ... outdated design principles the rest of the world has long soured on. These gated communities, mostly located outside the city centre, exacerbate China's urban sprawl. And ecologically speaking, they're a total disaster: water heavy, land intensive and deeply car dependent, they replicate some of the most problematic urban design practices.'

Part of the problem with China's more uncreative new cities derives from the way that land is sectioned off and sold. When blazing a new suburb, a local government will generally lay out a grid of four- to eight-lane highways and then sell the 500 × 500 square-metre lots between them to developers. The developers then tend to fill each square with singular apartment complexes, which are walled off from the street like fortresses. All too often, entire city districts build on this model become not much more than square palisades lined up for miles and miles, only giving way for a shopping mall or two.

The super-block movement also has a social impact. 'As the Chinese create more and more super-blocks of apartments and giant shopping centres, they're destroying a whole stratum of their traditional walkable society', Peter Calthorpe, an American architect, observed in an interview with *Fortune*. 'The Chinese used to live on the streets in wonderfully social ways, being able to stroll or ride their bikes to cafés and small shops' (Dumaine 2012). The traditional neighbourhoods and villages of China are full of life, talk, mahjong, children playing, laundry drying, food cooking, old ladies singing – people in the streets hanging out with family and friends with the front doors of their homes wide open. When those old, street-level homes are bulldozed and replaced with modern high-rise apartment complexes these close-knit communities often fail to make the transition. The contrast between the amount of open socializing that takes place in a traditional-style Chinese neighbourhood and in a high-rise is startling. 'We go into our apartments to hide', a young woman from Taizhou once told me.

One characteristic of China's modern planned cities is that they are generally built from the centre out. Elaborate, sometimes massive, downtown areas with central parks and public squares, monuments, government buildings, shopping malls and exhibition centres are completed ahead of essentials such as housing, schools and hospitals that actually sustain a population. This isn't a glitch in the system, but part of the plan. Building these new downtown cores essentially hammers in the piton that the rest of the city can hang off; as interest grows and companies and developers move in, new cities are provisioned with more and more elements, and eventually become inhabitable urban centres.

No matter how holistically designed they are, all planned cities eventually become organic entities. As time goes on unforeseen problems arise, technologies evolve, and the society's tastes and desires change. Before long, even the most singularly planned, all-encompassing new city breaks down and fractures as new, incongruous elements are added within the frame of what was once the grand design.

The cities of the future

'Environmental degradation in China has now become so severe that it is no longer just an issue threatening public health but also poses a challenge to urban social stability', wrote Pow Choon Piew and Harvey Neo on ChinaDialogue.net. Statements such as this are not only very common, but are rarely contested. If China is going to pull off its urbanization movement and advance into the next stage of development while maintaining economic, political and social stability it needs to fix its cities. So flagship projects have spread across the country to serve as live beta tests in the search for the answer to China's urban conundrum and enable the country's cities to continue growing.

Ecocities

What is an ecocity? The World Ecocity Summit 2008 in San Francisco declared that an ecocity is

> an ecologically healthy city. Into the deep future, the cities in which we live must enable people to thrive in harmony with nature and achieve sustainable development. People-oriented ecocity development requires the comprehensive understanding of complex interactions between environmental, economic, political and socio-cultural factors based on ecological principles. Cities, towns and villages should be designed to enhance the health and quality of life of their inhabitants and maintain the ecosystems on which they depend.

While the World Bank's 'Eco2 Cities' report claimed that

> Ecological cities enhance the wellbeing of citizens and society through integrated urban planning and management that fully harnesses the benefit of ecological systems, and protects and nurtures these assets for future generations.

If any country is poised to lead the green urbanization movement, it's China. This may seem counter-intuitive, as the country has one of the worst environmental track records, but this is precisely why China is grasping so hard at alternatives: the people know their environment has been devastated, they know the air they breathe is hazardous and the water they drink poisonous, and many of those who have the cash are willing to pay for another option. So searching for green building models is not only more environmentally conscious but also profitable.

Meixi Lake Eco-City

I cannot go so far as to say that what I was looking at was a pristine, natural scene, but I can say that I was far outside of any city, in an area of lakes, rivers, farms, foothills and wide-open spaces. Geometric rice paddies fit together like a puzzle leading out to a wall of small green mountains. Farmers walked by pushing dilapidated, cockeyed carts filled with the day's harvest, along with farming tools and scrap. But this rural landscape of green, brown and blue will before long be turned into a massive city of black, white and grey. An ecocity will be built here.

Positioned just outside of Changsha, the capital of Hunan province, a benchmark of global urbanism is being built. They are calling it the Meixi Lake Eco-City, and it's a prime example of the futuristic, built-from-scratch, low-carbon cities that have become extremely popular in China. 'Meixi is an experiment in future city planning and building ... It's a kind of live test case', one of the city's chief designers stated. In February 2009, the Changsha municipal government unleashed a plan that would carve out 6.8 sq km of land in its rural outskirts for this trend-setting new city. Working in tandem with the municipal government is big real-estate developer Gale International and China Merchants Bank, which provided a US$1.6 billion loan to cover the first five years of construction. The New York architecture firm Kohn Pedersen Fox and the UK engineering firm Arup, the designers of the Sydney Opera House, were chosen to devise the master plan.

The Meixi Lake development is laid out in a horseshoe pattern around a 40-hectare, 4 km-long artificial lake. It will have canals crisscrossing and neatly separating the city's various business and residential sectors. The downtown area will be made up of a CBD, and will contain Changsha's first super-tall structures. The city's layout will be set around the central lake, and a network of canals will complement the radial street pattern, allowing people to commute by boat, thus reducing dependency on cars. The CBD will be a reduced traffic zone, and will contain trams and walkable streets. Some 180,000 residents are expected to live here, divided into 10,000-person sub-units, aptly named 'villages'. These residential clusters will all have unique looks and individual identities, their own shopping malls, and will be separated from each other by parks and waterways. Beyond that, the city will benefit from large amounts of green space, grey and black water systems, urban agriculture, cutting-edge cultural and entertainment centres, its own distributed energy plants, waste energy recovery systems, and as much strange, sci-fi architecture that can be packed in. The promotional materials for the development claim that it will blend the urban landscape with that of the surrounding mountains, lakes and parks – a difficult challenge for a city of skyscrapers.

I was standing on the bank of the massive man-made lake in the centre of the development. Construction crews were busy stacking up high-rise towers. It was hard to fathom that this place, where there had been nothing but peasants growing rice and cabbage for hundreds of years, would soon host one of the most technologically advanced cities the world has ever known. I watched an old woman gathering greens from her small garden, seemingly oblivious to the towers that were going up all around, even though the racket of jackhammers, backhoes and cranes drives home the reality of what is happening here.

Meixi Lake Eco-city is set to be completed by 2020, and property speculators and potential homebuyers are already flooding in. I walked into a real-estate showroom that had scale models of the neighbourhoods currently under construction. I watched as women with thousand-dollar handbags pointed at the plastic towers, selecting apartments that cost millions of renminbi like clothes in a shopping mall window, as their chubby husbands with gold wristwatches nodded obediently. The parking lot outside was an array of BMW, Mercedes, Lexus cars and SUVs; off to the side was a bright red Ferrari. Ecocities are playgrounds for China's rich.

Tianfu ecocity

Along with the numerous generic suburban cities it is building, China is also trying to do the opposite: building cities where no one needs a car. Outside of Chengdu, Sichuan province, a site has been cleared out for a self-contained, eco-friendly city that aims to reduce its environmental impact by using greener forms of energy, cutting down on waste, and running a public transportation system and urban network that are so good that the private car would be passé. The new city is called Tianfu; it was designed by the architecture firm Adrian Smith + Gordon Gill, and is being brought to life by the Beijing Vantone Real Estate Co., in partnership with the Chengdu municipal government – of course.

Tianfu is designed to provision its 80,000 residents with all the latest green features bundled into a 1.3 sq km satellite city that sits very much removed from the downtown core of Chengdu. Half of the streets will be for pedestrians only and the farthest distance between any two points will be a short fifteen-minute walk. If transportation is desired, electric shuttles zip along the main thoroughfares. Some 60 per cent of the city's space is reserved for agriculture and green open space, which includes a 480-acre buffer area that separates the city from any sprawl that may head its way. It has been estimated that Tianfu will cut energy usage by 48 per cent and water by 58 per cent, generate 60 per cent less carbon dioxide, and dish out 89 per cent less waste than a similar-size city in China. The city will use seasonal energy storage, which uses heat captured in the summer to warm homes in the winter. It has even dubbed its sewage treatment and power plant facility an 'eco-park'. As for energy, the designers have already ruled out solar, as Chengdu's pollution doesn't allow enough sunlight to break through. However, large buildings all will be decked out with windmills. Like Meixi Lake, Tianfu should be completed by 2020.

Sino-Singapore Tianjin Ecocity

The Sino-Singapore Tianjin Ecocity (SSTEC) is a little different from many of the other ecocities in China, as it's a joint venture between Singapore's Keppel Group and China's Tianjin TEDA Investment Holding Company. The Memorandum of Understanding for the 50/50 joint venture was signed between Singapore prime minister Lee Hsien Loong and Chinese premier Wen Jiabao in November 2007, and construction began soon after. China Development Bank put up a good deal of the cash; by May 2010 the project reputedly had about US$1.5 billion in registered capital.

SSTEC will occupy a 34.2 sq km site, 40 km from the centre of Tianjin, roughly 150 km from Beijing. It is ten minutes from the Tianjin Economic-Technological Development Area (TEDA) and is 10 km from the core of the Binhai New Area, a rapidly developing zone that includes the Manhattan-inspired Yujiapu CBD. The location of SSTEC is concurrently one of its strong points and a weakness. Although it is in the heart of a very dynamic development area, it is also wedged between the heavily industrialized Hangu and Tanggu districts, which have long been chemical manufacturing bases, with attendant pollution problems. This presents some rather large hurdles for a city whose main selling point is its clean environment.

The philosophy of SSTEC revolves around its being practical, scalable and, perhaps most important of all, replicable. It will include cutting-edge green technologies, such as thermal insulation, rainwater collection, sky gardens, and extensive use of solar power. The city is committed to a high air-quality standard; the water (50 per cent from desalination and recycling) can be drunk directly from the tap; every building meets green building standards; carbon emissions are not to exceed 150 tonnes per US$1 million of GDP; and geothermal, hydro and solar power will together account for 15 per cent of total energy used. There will also be an 'eco business park' which will contain the offices of global companies involved in all aspects of green engineering, renewable energy and environmental issues. SSTEC is intended as an experiment in city building that can be reproduced else-where around the world.

SSTEC has been called the most promising of China's ecoci-ties by environmental activist Wang Bao, and the city seems vastly more organized and less opaque than the many other similar experiments that China has tried before. To vitalize the city, a formal plan had been laid out to provide tax incentives for residents and companies, housing rebates, R&D start-up financing, as well as free schooling and lunches for children. Furthermore, 20 per cent of the housing will be publicly subsidized, jobs will be created within the city for at least 50 per cent of employable residents, and subsidies for businesses will be provided. Some 350,000 people are expected to inhabit this city by 2023. The first phase of the development were opened to residents in 2012. At present, this 3 sq km area houses around 6,000 people, which is fewer than the 10,000 expected, but enough to raise the city above ghost town status. The cost of housing here is currently US$1,300 per square metre, which is relatively low, especially for Tianjin. This city was designated a centre for China's animation, audiovisual and publishing industries, and over a thousand businesses have moved in, bringing with them registered capital in excess of US$10 billion and 4,000 jobs. As with many of China's new cities, the vitalization progress might seem slow when compared to the pace of construction. However, given that six years ago the place was nothing but an expanse of saline land, criticism in this regard carries no weight.

The ecocity gimmick?

The words 'eco' and 'city' together seem to be an oxymoron. If ecological well-being alone was truly its goal, China wouldn't be ploughing up thousands of square kilometres of agricultural fields, small villages, wooded areas and foothills to build new ecocities. 'It's difficult everywhere, all over the world, to develop something like cities in a sustainable way', reflected Fanny Hoffman-Loss, the principal architect of the Nanhui ecocity, which sits on the far edge of Shanghai's Pudong district. 'So in many cases it just ends up being some marketing thing. On the other hand, that's how things start... it's a step in the right direction.'

If these ecocities seem like a marketing ploy, it's because to an extent they are. Ecocities garner far more positive attention than normal cities, and positive attention is often a healthy precursor to profit, and, in the case of Chinese officials, promotion. Add the subsidies that have been allotted to ecological development by the central government as part of its 12th five-year plan and increased environmental awareness across the population, and the impetus to 'build green' is greater than ever before. Almost 300 ecocities are either being built or are in the planning stage across China. As of now only 2 per cent of new cities in China carry the 'eco' brand, but this number is expected to rise to 50 per cent. These green building initiatives are called experiments, but their pace of proliferation around the country has been so rapid that by the time adequate results are available hundreds will already be built and functioning. To date not a single ecocity in China has been fully built and populated. To put it bluntly, there is no data available to assess whether they live up to their name.

This raises the question of whether these places are truly being built to establish a new green urbanism or simply represent cash cows for local governments and developers – an excuse to build yet another new city. There is no established standard as to what qualifies a place to be an ecocity, and the green label is conveniently being slapped on all types of new developments. In an article entitled 'How to Spot a Fake Ecocity' (in ChinaDialogue. net), Li Xun, secretary of the Chinese Society for Urban Studies, claimed that only one in five of China's ecocities 'actually match low-carbon or ecological ideals'. He posed the question, 'Are we turning our backs on low-carbon and ecological ideals, all the while believing we are moving towards them? Are they fake low-carbon schemes? Or are there even cases that are actively anti-low carbon, anti-eco? Well, yes, there are.' Bianca Bosker, the author of *Original Copies*, for her part, is clear that '"green" architecture has become a compelling brand in the marketplace, although many of these so-called "eco" communities offer little more than the same sprawling McMansions under a different name.' Ecocities seem to be a new form of cover that enables China's urbanization drive to continue on into the future, a way of mitigating criticism that the movement is laying waste to the country's environment. In the end, no matter how 'eco' these ecocities are, they are nevertheless cities: they still pollute, they still suck up resources, they still consume a massive amount of material, and they demand even more infrastructure. The carbon footprint of a city is never slight. Perhaps most detrimental of all is the fact that, rather than ecologically redesigning buildings in existing cities, China's ecocities are being built in places where there has never been urbanization before. There is nothing more 'ecological' than the countryside these ecocities destroy. However, there is also truth in the common rebuttal that says if China is going to build a new city anyway, it may as well be an ecocity.

Central Business Districts – everywhere

I once thought that a city building a new central business district (CBD) was a monumental undertaking. My previous knowledge told me that only global centres of finance – places like Manhattan, London, Paris, Tokyo, Dubai, Shanghai and Beijing – had CBDs. However, when I began travelling around China visiting its new cities and large-scale urban developments I found myself in more specially built financial districts than I could imagine any country ever needing. The USA has two CBDs, in New York and Chicago; a handful of other economically prosperous nations have one; and most countries don't have any at all; yet China now has dozens of CBDs spread across the country.

Central business districts do not have a very long tradition in China. In the early 1990s, when China's new city movement first began raising its head, China had no CBDs. But then Shanghai began developing the Lujiazui business district in Pudong. Following its success, Beijing and Guangzhou revealed plans for their own CBDs. But it didn't stop there: many other cities started emulating the Pudong model, and before long an epidemic of financial districts swept the country. Nearly every city now wanted a CBD, and many began building them whether they were needed or not. In 2003 the Ministry of Construction tried to get a handle on the CBD building boom and conducted a nationwide survey. It found that thirty-six cities had projects to develop financial districts in the works. In addition to Shanghai, Beijing and Guangzhou, almost all of the big cities in the country were rolling them out – Chongqing, Tianjin, Shenyang, Jinan, Zhengzhou, Xi'an, Chengdu, Wuhan, Nanjing, Hangzhou, Dalian, Ningbo and Shenzhen. But perhaps a more significant finding was that many smaller cities, such as Xiangyang, Huangshi, Shaoxing, Wenzhou, Yiwu and Foshan, to name just a few, were also building full-scale CBDs. This was viewed as a problem because it was felt that these small cities lacked both the demand for such a development as well as the capital to get them properly built and functioning. At an initial investment of US$1.23 billion on average, CBDs in China don't come cheap, and at the time of the Ministry of Construction's report it was calculated that, based on annual revenue, some of the cities were looking at a period of between ten and twenty-five years just to pay for them (Wei 2005). Nevertheless the survey ultimately had little impact, and the CBD building boom continued. Hence in 2014 the CBD is a near ubiquitous landmark in China's cities. Most mid- to large-sized cities have one – even lowly Taizhou in Jiangsu province apparently felt that it wouldn't be complete without its very own central business district. 'Most of China's major cities are trying to develop new CBDs, sometimes two new CBDs, and even three new CBDs', observed Frank Chen, CBRE's executive director for China, in an interview with *China Economic Review*. Shanghai plans to eventually have at least three CBDs on the east, west and south sides of its urban core, while Beijing envisions four business districts, one at each compass point. As discussed earlier, Wuxi started building one CBD, paused, and then started building another one in a different location.

'When the concept of Central Business Districts (CBDs) was borrowed from the West in the early 1990s ... local governments welcomed the idea with great enthusiasm, viewing it as a cure-all solution to remake the morbid built environment inherited from the socialist years', Xuefei Ren wrote in her book *Urban China*. Business districts in China usually comprise an array of towers for financial institutions, multinational corporations, general office space, luxury hotels, upper-end apartment complexes, and, in major cities, often embassies and consulates.

An incredible number of cities in China are vying to become the financial hub of their region or even of the entire country. Having a CBD has almost become a requisite for a city to be taken seriously as an economic and political contender. It is seen as a vital ingredient in the aspirations of small cities to become big cities, which is often the goal. As all administrative regions in China are essentially in competition with each other for investment, industry, favourable central government policies and talent, and all officials are essentially in competition with each other for promotion, the role of the CBD has been deflected from its original function. CBDs now offer much more than just a place for financial industries, multinational corporations and SOEs to coalesce; they provide an iconic new image for the cities they are built in, giving them a new skyline of sparkling grey skyscrapers that serves to make any place appear modern, internationalized and wealthy. CBDs once gave municipalities an advantage over their rivals, but now that they are so common it is necessary to have one just to keep up. As an August 2014 Jone Lang LaSalle report remarks: 'The "if you build it, they will come" economic development model has become broken, as the model only works if "it" has not already been built somewhere nearby and there is sufficient demand.'

Be that as it may, there are solid financial incentives for cities to run a successful CBD. When a municipality sells residential land it only receives tax revenue once in the entire seventy-year span of the lease, but when it sells land for commercial development it takes an annual tax revenue cut. Beyond that, financial districts have the power to attract businesses to a city, which further increases the tax take of a municipal government.

Many of the ghost cities in China are CBDs that are either just getting started or have become stagnant. While the vacancy rate of Beijing's Chaoyang CBD is just 5 per cent and Shanghai's Lujiazui fell to 2.4 per cent in 2014, financial districts in most of the country's other cities are not doing so well. The vacancy rate in tier-two cities is around 21 per cent on average, which is double what is generally felt to be healthy. In Chengdu's CBD the vacancy rate is 44 per cent, and this is before the city adds over 1.5 million square metres of office space as the development expands. The full scale of vacant office space cannot be known, however, as a large portion of CBDs in China are still in the process of being built or expanded, and the office capacity that they will eventually create has not yet flooded the market. Tianjin's still unopened Yujiapu CBD, for example, aims to provide 3.04 million square metres of office space by 2020. So it is clear that China's CBD oversupply can only get a lot worse.

Zhujiang

Zhujiang New Area is now the financial heart of Guangzhou. Some who live there now refer to it as the city's centre. This new financial district wasn't always so vibrant. Construction on Zhujiang began in the early 1990s as Guangzhou tried to match Shanghai punch for punch by adding what was then a novel idea: a CBD. While Shanghai's Lujiazui sprouted up from the Pudong mucklands relatively quickly, Zhujiang floundered for over a decade. The project went through successive starts and stops, and at one point was looking as if it was going to be abandoned altogether, leaving behind one of the largest white elephants in history. But with the advent of the 2010 Asian Games focus returned to the project. Guangzhou decided to base the major sporting event in the new district. Before long, supertalls were sprouting out of the moist soil on the banks of the Pearl River. Beneath them luxury shopping malls, verdant parks and world-class landmarks – including Zaha Hadid's opera house and the Canton Tower, the world's fifth largest free-standing structure – were built along an iconic 1.5 km central plaza.

For a long period the grandiose structures of the new CBD appeared to have been built on false pretences. They stood virtually empty, as local businesses and financial institutions were not convinced that they should move in. As Paul Wells, the political editor for Canada's *Maclean's Magazine*, blogged in February of 2012: 'The only thing missing was people... It's a fake opera house across the park from a fake shopping mall next to a fake hotel in a fake neighbourhood designed to snow gullible foreigners, not 100 km from villages whose residents live in grinding poverty' (Wells 2012). The place was a virtual ghost city, a place built for a demand that hadn't materialized.

It is now mid-July 2014, and I have visited the Zhujiang CBD three times in the past three weeks. I have to report that little seems to be out of the ordinary in terms of population, business density and street life when compared with other large business districts in China. While many skyscrapers are still under construction, what's there is being utilized. Most of Guangzhou's banks and a large number of its SOEs relocated there, as what just a couple of years ago was a showy monument to opulence and excess has become the central axis of China's fourth most populated city.

Such transitions can happen so quickly in China because they are often the direct consequence of government decrees, rather than the outcome of the gradual evolution of urbanization and a market economy. When local governments in China build large-scale new districts there is often an interim period when they face off against the businesses and institutions that the real estate was created for. It is also not uncommon for businesses and residents to be extremely keen to buy up available office space and residential units, but very reluctant to move in. This is for good reason: new districts and cities tend to be built in the middle of nowhere, initially lacking good public transportation links and proper facilities. So they buy property and simply wait. As a developer in Nanhui, a nearly deserted new city 60 km outside of Shanghai, once told me: 'The only question here is when?'

In big cities like Guangzhou, local government policies can act as triggers to make 'when' come a little sooner. Zhujiang was vitalized in a similar way as almost every other large-scale CBD in China: the government forcibly moved the businesses and institutions they control. This they did with SOEs, government banks, administrative departments and customs offices, and they offered attractive incentives to multinational corporations and domestic private companies. A 3-hectare lot was even given to the US Consulate.

The idea is to provide a framework of infrastructure, then plant a catalyst of commerce and activity from which a viable economic and social base can develop. By the time this occurs everything is usually primed for market forces to take over. In

China's big cities, local governments have the power to move large numbers of people and capital, and this system works. Zhujiang now sits at the crossroads of three major subway lines; it is the new centre of Guangzhou.

Industrially themed cities

Along with ecocities and CBDs, China is building more than its share of industrially themed cities. These are essentially entire new urban developments that are constructed for a single industry. For example, Xinyu, in Jiangxi province, was built for the solar-power industry. This is actually a natural form of organization in China, as industries of a feather have always had the tendency to flock together. It's a practical strategy: locating in one place everything an industry needs to function makes for more efficient and less costly production.

China Medical City

China Medical City (CMC) is in no way a misnomer. In 2005, a 30 sq km area north just of the Yangtze River between Shanghai and Nanjing was marked off and designated for one of the largest medical research centres in China. It sits in Taizhou, between its Hailing and Gaogang districts, in an area where there is, quite literally, nothing else. Well, nothing else anymore. The agricultural villages that dotted this landscape for centuries had already been demolished and cleared away, their residents forced out, paid off and relocated elsewhere, their fertile fields ploughed up, levelled off, and neatly parcelled into vacant dirt lots: the ideal canvas to paint a new city. And a new city is exactly what CMC is meant to be.

This place is a new city specially made for medical and pharmaceuticals research and production. It is set to be home to 100,000 residents employed in the biosciences. Imagine an area half the size of Manhattan that's full of scientists, lab techs and pharmaceuticals dealers. The vision is to make CMC a global epicentre for the biosciences that would integrate all stages of the industry into a single location. The initiative is not unlike a medical-themed version of what the Pearl River Delta (aka The World's Factory) was in the 1990s and early 2000s, where every element needed for manufacturing was brought together in one place.

The CMC was an all-or-nothing, larger-than-the-largest, type of project of the kind that China has become known for over the past fifteen years. RMB100 billion (in excess of US$16 billion) was earmarked for the development. It was as though a political demigod had whipped out a map of the country, put his finger down on the eastern stretches of the Yangtze River, and proclaimed 'Let there be a medical city!' Looked at superficially, this isn't far from the truth. Taizhou just happens to be the hometown of Hu Jintao, who was the president of China at the time CMC was started. Mr Hu played a major role during the medical city's early stages and remained a staunch supporter throughout his time in office. The project is also firmly backed by Li Yunchao, China's current vice president, who was the Party boss of Jiangsu province when the CMC was first conceived.

Yet magnitude alone isn't the only factor that makes this medical complex stand out from similar ones in Hangzhou, Shanghai and Beijing: in 2009 Taizhou's CMC was put fully under the direction of the central government. This means that provincial, prefectural and municipal governments are bypassed when it comes to decision-making or financing. The CMC has its own local government, judicial precinct and police department. For the businesses that operate here, the advantage is clear: because this is a national-level biomedical facility, companies can leapfrog multiple bureaucratic levels and submit their drugs to the CFDA (China's drug regulation body) directly for approval.

The plan is to turn China Medical City into a completely self-sustaining new city. It is divided up into research and production, health care, education, business and residential zones. Skyscrapers of a new CBD are also sprouting up in the development's eastern sector. In 2014, nine years after construction began, CMC was rolling – the scale models and renderings giving way to laboratories, facilities, hospitals, factories and high-rises. But the place is still only a third built, barely covering 11 of the 30 square kilometres allotted to it. If one looks out from this development in any direction one sees seemingly endless expanses of cleared lots.

There is no mistaking this place. A large disk-shaped building, designed to look like a skin cell, looms near the main entrance. 'Inside the halls are made to look like blood vessels', a CMC representative told me. Across the street a giant sign that says 'National medical hi-tech development zone technological enterprise accelerator' hovers above a giant laboratory. In case one has trouble figuring out what this mouthful means, on the ground right next to the main entrance three 5-foot-high letters rise from a flower garden. They say 'C-M-C' – China Medical City, a name that says it all.

Once inside CMC one sees innumerable monotonous, blank-faced, cube-like buildings standing together in tight clusters. A strict grid of super-blocks that stretch for a kilometre between intersections is the design here. Scattered within them are labs and factories with names like Walvax, Takeda, Guodan Biological, Beikie Biotech, Bio Perfect Technologies, AstraZeneca and Edding Pharma.

On the ground, CMC has the look and feel of a ghost city. A conspicuous stillness pervades the place: there is little

movement, not much traffic, and many of the buildings appear
from the outside to be deserted. The quietude is conspicuous.
One might wonder if there are actually any people here at all,
if this isn't one colossal stage set – but then one catches sight
of a solitary tech in a lab coat scurrying from one white cube
to another. It is said that around 20,000 people currently live
here; of these 4–5,000 are Nanjing Chinese Medicine University
students, who were drafted in as part of the vitalization plan.

I went into Starbucks. Where there's a new city or district in
China there will be a Starbucks. The company's circular green
and white logo has become emblematic of the country's urbanization drive, with branches moving in to China's new outposts
of progress, often before the cranes and backhoes even move
out – serving overpriced coffee, sweet tea drinks and pastries to
relocated white-collar workers, exiled students and the modern
homesteaders who gradually trickle into the new city.

I asked the girl behind the counter how she ended up in such
a far-flung new development.

'My company sent me here', she told me.

'What, Starbucks?' I exclaimed in surprise, unable to check
an exasperated laugh.

She nodded in the affirmative, and then explained how she
was dispatched from her home city of Qingdao in Shandong
province across the country to the CMC. Starbucks in China
trains its baristas and then sends them off to various posts around
the country where they are needed. All too often they are sent out
to pioneer towns: new cities and urban districts in the transition
stage of development, between being constructed and coming to
life. That is, they are sent out to places like China Medical City.

'Do you like living here?' I asked the young woman.

'It is very quiet here', she responded, 'so sometimes I like it.
But often I hate it. Every time I want to go do something like
shopping I have to go all the way into the city, and I don't have a
car. There is nothing here.'

'What is there to do here?' I asked as she was pouring my coffee.

'There is a restaurant, some places to go shopping, a bar, Starbucks, and nothing.'

It was true. This place may as well have been called China Medical Island for how connected it is to the outside world. It is billed as being within the bounds of Taizhou, a city of 5 million people, but is really a completely independent urban centre separated from the city's other districts by miles of farmland and construction sites.

'Not that many people live here, right?' I asked the barista.

She said that this was true, but added that a big foreign biomed company was moving in soon, so more people were on the way. I couldn't help but feel that this was the kind of rumour that keeps this place going. It's the kind of talk that resonates through all frontier towns: the whispered excitement that something big is always on the verge of happening.

I met Chou on one of the winding cobblestone streets in front of a coffee shop of more local distinction. He was the owner of the place, which was called Lava Café. He was, he told me, a Taiwanese architect who had spent ten years in the USA studying at the University of Chicago and working in California. Then in 2007 he took a job as a project manager at an interior design firm in Shanghai. It was here that he was picked up by the radar of talent scouts at CMC, who were impressed by his work enough to invite him over to lead a project.

Chou was around 35 years old. He spoke American English with hardly a trace of a foreign accent, emphasized with an excessive use of colloquialisms – 'dude' and 'man' peppered his speech. 'I'm kind of a hybrid', he admitted. He was exactly the type of multicultural, internationalized individual that China's new cities tend to attract.

'Is the rent free here?' I asked him as we sat back in some chairs out on the café's patio, knowing that it's normal for businesses big and small to be lured into China's new cities with this incentive.

'We get two years free', he replied.

After that he will need to pay around US$540 per month.

'What do you think about the progress of the CMC? Is it stagnant or doomed to fail?' I asked directly.

Chou just stared ahead calmly and said simply, 'It's a long journey; lets hope we can survive it.' He paused for a moment before adding, 'You cannot have high expectations. It's a long-term thing.'

This may as well have been the mantra for China's entire urbanization movement.

'Do you think they can pull it off?' I asked.

'There's no turning back now', he replied quickly with a laugh. 'It's been a rocky road. You always have to adapt. You have to always be learning how to do everything better. It hasn't come to the time to reach a conclusion, but right now it's acceptable.'

'You seem very hopeful and optimistic.'

'Those who aren't are gone already', he replied with a laugh.

That was true. I told him the saga of David Wilson.

In 2009 David Wilson was invited to start up a contract manufacturing business at the CMC to produce globally compliant pharmaceuticals in line with FDA and EU regulations. He responded to the opportunity with an enthusiastic 'yes'.

'From March 2009 to June 2010 I spent sixteen months working on the proposal to have CMC fund a biologics contract manufacturing company', he told me. 'Once the JV [joint venture] was approved I spent a year living and working in CMC.'

He was to provide the know-how and the CMC would take care of the rest. On the promise of US$100 million of funding and a 20,000 sq ft facility the JV was born. He brought over his American team and got to work.

The Americans quickly discovered that the Chinese do business their own way. The CMC admitted that they had overextended their resources. As Wilson wrote on his blog, 'every invoice and paycheck has to go through government processing so it can juggle its books to keep everything running, which is more bureaucratic and byzantine than you can imagine … One has to become the perpetual "squeaky wheel" to get what they need, and it can be exhausting and distracting.' Eventually, the bottom fell out. 'The CMC funding was only on paper and they stopped paying me in June 2011', he recalled. 'The project was reassigned to a Chinese pharma company and the US team left. After completing all milestones and performance under budget, the project began with enthusiasm and finished with disappointment.'

Basically, the CMC used the expertise of David and his American team to set up a monoclonals facility, something CMC wanted but couldn't do for themselves, and then, when it was up and running and a Chinese team was adequately trained, the Americans were shown the door.

As Wilson later wrote on his blog: 'I didn't expect the government, with all that trade surplus money, would renege on their contractual obligations, so everyone, be advised … My advice to those considering working in China is to fully understand the business environment and perspective, because they are very different than in the West, plus always retain your leverage in business relationships. Once they disappear, you are gone.'

'Foreigners can't do business in China', Chou snorted after I finished the story. 'They can't understand how it works. It's like a hustle game; if you start dancing in political games you're going to dig a hole you can't get out of.'

'What are the problems that the CMC is currently facing?' I asked.

'Not enough people', Chou replied simply.

It was true. The key to the success of this incredibly ambitious project is to attract foreign businesses and entice them to relocate here. One of the major problems with this has proved to be the fact that not many highly skilled foreigners are standing in line to go live in a partially built intentional city in the middle of the Jiangsu agricultural plains. 'If CMC has an Achilles heel it is that Taizhou is not nearly as cosmopolitan as Shanghai or even Hangzhou', ran a *PharmAsia News* report on 11 August 2011. The story continued by stating that 'recruiting and retaining talent will be a challenge … Epitomics, for instance, moved a team of 15 employees from Hangzhou to CMC, but only five have stayed.'

Nevertheless, the CMC's developers remain confident that their project will be able to compete with the more established biomedical facilities in the country. 'They're maxed out', one foreign builder working at CMC told me about Hangzhou's and Suzhou's medical centres; 'they have no more space to grow.' The CMC, on the other hand, is only a third built, and is surrounded by unchecked miles of potential development land. Indeed, there are few physical barriers to growth here – which is one of the prime advantages of building a new city in the proverbial middle of nowhere.

Duplitecture and the search for identity

Throughout their history the Chinese have absorbed other cultural traditions, technologies, belief systems, even invaders, and made them Chinese. It is no different in the modern era. Starting in the early 2000s, classical Western architecture became very popular throughout China. Suddenly, full-scale European-style towns began popping up across the country. The imitation of grandiose Western architecture has become so common that it could almost be considered a new style of Chinese architecture. Vanke, China's largest private real-estate developer, estimates that two-thirds of its properties are built in a Western style.

'As the number of residential developments grew, so too did the prevalence of China's Western-style copycat architecture: in a crowded market, developers looked for ways to brand their communities and set them apart in the eyes of an increasingly discriminating set of homebuyers', Bianca Bosker, the author of *Original Copies*, the definitive book on China's duplitecture, told me. 'Since the Baroque, Mediterranean or Beverly Hills-themed neighbourhoods could sell for more money – and more quickly – than their more generic counterparts, more and more of them appeared.'

Yujiapu Replica

Apparently not content with allowing New Yorkers to remain the sole beneficiaries of their city's charms, a group of enterprising developers and government officials have engaged upon the most extensive and ambitious knock-off in human history: the creation of a Manhattan-themed financial district – in Tianjin, China. The bounds of geography, culture and history are no match for a rising superpower that takes architectural designs and urban layouts from around the world as though window-shopping in a mall. Significantly, when it's finished Yujiapu will be larger than Manhattan's business district.

Although I refer to Yujiapu as a Manhattan financial district (FiDi) knock-off, it is not an exact replica. Whereas some buildings are being cloned and the theme is overtly 'Manhattan', the layout and finer aspects of the design are different. One major deviation from the original is that Yujiapu's developers have added a Central Park-like green space in the middle of their creation, whereas the actually Manhattan financial district is pretty much a contiguous koosh ball of skyscrapers. *The Atlantic* notes other marked differences: 'A few of Yujiapu's features are originals: an urban park on a whale-shaped island; an underground strip of high-end stores; and China's first three-tier, underground train station, where bullet trains will shoot commuters off to Beijing as well as Tianjin, a nearby boom town of almost eleven million people.'

The cold, no-frills monoliths of Communist-era architecture no longer warm many hearts in China. A country that for two generations constructed only block-shaped, grey buildings perhaps deserves some critical leeway when the creativity valve is released and out burst some of the most outlandish buildings and development projects the world has ever known. Freed from the strictures of tradition, hurtling into the future, architectural anarchy is the rule in modern China.

Having said that, it is my impression that the Manhattan theme is more or less a promotional gimmick to put and keep this project in the spotlight. For this place to prosper it needs to attract both national and international companies. It needs to create a buzz, push some buttons, sound a few sirens, trip a couple of alarms. Journalists are animated about Yujiapu not because it is intended to be northern China's financial hub and represents the overdevelopment, overspending and overoptimism that characterize this phase of the country's development, but because it is being built to look like Manhattan. In fact, I probably would not have visited Yujiapu if it was merely another big Chinese financial development on the brink of bankruptcy; indeed very few of us would hear about this place if it wasn't a replica. In an odd twist of logic, by copying a famous city Yujiapu made itself unique.

The Chinese have appropriated traditional styles of architecture, adapted them to the modern era, claimed them for themselves, and use them for their *own* monumentality. This copycat behaviour may seem like a pathetic attempt at flattery to the people of the countries whose architecture is being ripped off, but that's not what it is meant to do. Building copies of the great architectural achievements of other cultures has been something the Chinese have done since the Qin dynasty (221–206 BCE). 'By appropriating the monumental trappings of power from distant places and times', wrote Jack Carlson in *Foreign Policy*, 'the Chinese do not merely place their own country on a symbolic par with historical Western superpowers, but suggest that China has mastered and transcended their levels of achievement.' To take the great architectural achievements of powerful cultures past and present and copy them is a way of saying 'See, they're not so great after all' – or, perhaps more accurately, 'we're just as good as they are'. As Bosker explained,

> By re-creating Paris, China isn't paying homage to France, it's celebrating China's progress, deep pockets and power. Just as the architecture of their enemies was transposed by China's pre-modern, imperial rulers to show off their strength, these reproductions are meant to tell the world, and China's own population, that China is so mighty it can figuratively rearrange the universe and 'own' the landmarks the West holds most dear. China's duplitecture has a clear message to the world: Whatever you've accomplished, we can do, too – only bigger and faster.

For all that, there are other reasons for the boom in duplitecture, such as its uncanny ability to show status. The end of the Mao era created a vacuum of status symbols in China, so when the country opened up and the money began flowing in, there were no established ways to show off the new status that many people were attaining. So Western styles filled the void. The idea of the West was associated with wealth, so it is easy to see how this symbolism was transferred to architecture. 'In China, the Western "brand" still enjoys certain connotations of luxury, sophistication, wealth, power and prestige, and the home buyers who move into the fake Frances or Californias believe their themed neighbourhood will show them to be successful and worldly', Bosker told me. 'The homeowners aren't just buying shelter when they buy into these theme-towns. They're also buying the appearance of success. The duplitecture can serve the same purpose as a Chanel logo on a designer purse: they're status symbols that are meant to convey an air of worldliness and accomplishment for the people living within.' Most of China's 4 million+ wealthy households acquired this status within a single generation; like the nouveau riche everywhere, they are prone to flaunt their socio-economic ascension. Address is the biggest indicator of class in China; living in a Western-themed town or an ecocity is to show a social identity at the upper level.

Hallstatt

I descended a hill and rounded a bend, said hello to a security guard decked out in an overly fancy Germanic-influenced military uniform, then walked out onto a precipice that overlooked Hallstatt. The church's towering steeple was the centrepiece of this quaint little European hamlet, which sat on the bank of an artificial lake within the contours of an artificial hill. In fact, the entire place was artificial, from the landscape to the buildings to the people. I wasn't in Hallstatt, Austria, but Hallstatt, China – the 1:1 scale copy of the UNESCO World Heritage site in Guangdong province.

The Chinese are known for their skill at making knock-off handbags, apparel, electronics, watches, and just about everything else, but this was a knock-off of an entire town, which clearly took the country's propensity for copying to an entirely new level. Street for street, brick for brick, fixture for fixture, facade for facade, they built a nearly exact replica of an entire historic village. Old European hamlets may not be copyrightable, but China has demonstrated that they are definitely copyable. To put it simply, this has never been done before. Never before in human history has one country built a full-scale copy of a place in another country. Hallstatt, China is the mother of all knock-offs.

Just as they go about copying the design of a handbag or a piece of fashionable clothing by studying photos in magazines and catalogues, teams of Chinese urban planners went to Hallstatt and physically measured and photographed the old town's proportions, compiling it all into workable blueprints. This was all done in secret; Austria had no idea what was happening until well after Hallstatt the Second began rising out of the dust in Guangdong. In fact, the copycat village was only discovered when the Chinese set of blueprints was carelessly left behind in an Austrian hotel in 2011.

China's Hallstatt was created with an investment of nearly $1 billion. The reproduction village is intended to act as a beacon to lure the wealthy from other parts of the Pearl River Delta to purchase the vast array of villas for sale there.

I hopped off a bus in Boluo, which is just outside of Huizhou, flagged down a young guy in the street, and showed him a photo of the village I'd downloaded onto my smartphone. He looked at the snapshot of a row of life-sized gingerbread houses and pointed me to the edge of town. A short motorcycle taxi ride later, along a mud-strewn, unfinished road, I was staring down at the replica village itself.

It clearly wasn't some designer handbag type of knock-off;

this place was copycat perfection. The Austrian Hallstatt is wedged between a hill and a lake; the Chinese one is too. The resemblance to the real Hallstatt goes down to the smallest detail. There were flowers everywhere; the sound of birdsong was playing in the streets through hidden speakers; the streets themselves were paved with bricks laid in semi-circular patterns; the fountain in the centre was an identical match; the *Sound of Music* soundtrack, playing on an endless loop, could be heard everywhere: 'Doe, a deer, a female deer...' Cafés and bars had their renminbi prices masquerading as euros: €58 for a cup of coffee?

The buildings were near perfect copies of the originals. When one studies photos of the Austrian Hallstatt and the Chinese Hallstatt side by side, their dimensions, shapes, facades and even colour are almost identical. Even the tapering alleys and off-kilter positioning of the buildings were reproduced with precision.

The area surrounding Hallstatt village centre was what this project was really all about: a massive housing development. Covering the hills around the lake are Western-style villas of various types and sizes. The cloned village is just the marketing bait to attract media attention and lure in homebuyers.

Although Guangdong's Hallstatt is the first example of an exact replica of a European locale in China, it is not the first Western-style town to be built here. Old World European look-alike towns are springing up all around the country: Shanghai has its Thames Town, Taizhou has Oriental Windsor Village, and other British, German and Italian imitation developments have been popping up with great frequency. Yet what these places have in common, other than the fact that their architecture is copied, is that they are all nearly deserted. These developments represent a new phenomenon in China: Western-themed ghost towns, the perfect marketing ploy for the Chinese real-estate speculation market.

As I walked through the streets of the Chinese Hallstatt I could not help but think that this place may be destined to meet a similar fate as many of China's other Western-themed towns: built just to fall into ruin. Notwithstanding the magnificent faux Austrian buildings that were copied close to perfection, it all came over as manifestly lifeless. The only people there were portrait photographers utilizing the exotic town as a backdrop.

Until relatively recently, Hallstatt, Austria was not even a blip in Chinese consciousness. In 2005, only fifty tourists from China were recorded as visiting the village. Since then, however, the place has assumed a sort of mythic status for the Chinese. With an increased interest in Europe and old European styles, Hallstatt – with its mountainous scenery, fresh air, bounteous nature, strict environmental laws, and a populous committed to clean living – has become a metaphor for everything that China isn't. Chinese tourists very quickly began flocking to this alpine retreat in droves.

Hallstatt in Guangdong is an attempt to capitalize on this romance. It's an attempt to provide an escape from China within the country's national borders; it is a reaction to the crowded, polluted big cities that the Chinese have surrounded themselves with – it's an escape from the nightmare of their own making. There is a growing demand in China for nature-conscious, green, less polluted, healthier environs, and this is what many of the country's Western-themed towns claim to provide. But, ironically, the escape that is being sold is little other than the same urbanization wearing a different suit of clothes.

I asked some of the nearby residents what they thought of the copycat development. A college student from Huizhou looked at me quizzically before replying, 'If there are two of them it means that it is not so special.' A portrait photographer working at the site was more forthright: 'It's a fake', he said boldly while curling his lip. 'There are no people, there is no culture. It's just a fake.'

There is another reason for the Western replica boom that is a little more pragmatic: the developments are attractive and are often pleasant places to live. They are the polar opposite of the typical Chinese city. Whereas the urban landscapes across China are characterized by virtually identical, block-shaped high-rises made to house as many people as possible, invariably standing behind the high walls of their respective compounds arranged in neat, monotonous super-blocks, the Western-themed towns stand in absolute contrast. Their dwellings are typically villas or low-rise apartments designed for a low population density. The downtown areas have intentionally winding roads lined with trees and flanked by wide sidewalks. There are often hillocks and ponds built just to be admired. These are places that are built especially to stroll in. I have to admit that they are agreeable places to be.

Conclusion

Difference sells. When it comes down to it these places are more of a marketing tactic than any kind of social statement. They sell, so developers make more and more of them. Nevertheless, this grasping for status and wealth seems to have been the undoing of many of China's Western replica towns. In general the properties sell quickly, but usually to buyers who treat them as investments to resell later or novelties to show off to their friends, rather than as actual homes. These places can be seen as collectors' items: their perceived high value inhibits actual use. And, like an autographed football or an old piece of furniture, they sit on display, their function betrayed by their representation of wealth.

China is a country that is searching for its own identity; this is demonstrated nowhere more poignantly than in the architecture of new cities. China's architects, engineers and city planners have been turning cityscapes throughout the country into surreal locations, throwing up monumental works in styles from the West, the East, the past and the future. This architectural mish-mash, involving replication, innovation and experimentation, suggests a nation developing through adolescence. 'Before it was popular for China to copy more developed counties. We used to think that everything that was foreign was good. But now we don't want to copy; it's not good to copy', a Chinese resident of Gaoqiao's New Netherlands Dutch Town told me. 'I think all of China is looking for an identity', proclaimed Shanghai-based architect Fanny Hoffman-Loss. 'Everybody is looking for something; it can't all be money. You need to find something to be proud of in your culture, so architecture is one part of this search for identity.'

Throughout China, for every Meixihu or Tianfu or Thames Town there are a hundred run-of-the-mill, standard, cookie-cutter developments and new towns being neatly planted in between perfectly rectangular superblocks. That is, these fancy themed towns are the exception, not the rule, in China's new cities. Their main value is perhaps in the influence that they will have on the future standard of Chinese architecture.

SEVEN

Powering the new China

Sails move with the wind.
Tortoise and snake are still.
Great plans are afoot:
A bridge will fly to span the north and south,
Turning a deep chasm into a thoroughfare;
Walls of stone will stand upstream to the west
To hold back Wushan's clouds and rain
Till a smooth lake rises in the narrow gorges.
The Mountain Goddess if she is still there
Will marvel at a world so changed.

Mao Zedong, 'Swimming'

Rising with the tide of hundreds of new cities and thousands of new towns are seemingly endless numbers of power plants. Cities are electronic devices; they need to be plugged in. Manufacturing the energy to power these places is nearly as big an endeavour as building them. How China does this has a direct impact on the quality of life that can be had within them and how sustainable they eventually become. No matter how much money a city's residents have, no matter how many apartments, cars and possessions they've accumulated, the quality of life they can lead is stunted if they are poisoned daily while living in an environmental wasteland.

According to the World Bank, China's 731 million urban residents use three times more energy than those living in rural areas.

Therefore drastically increasing the urban population means a big boost in energy consumption. China's urban residents, on average, also spend twice as much money and buy far more goods and services than those in the countryside. This is, of course, by design, as expanding the domestic retail market is one of the stated goals of China's urbanization movement. But an environmental price comes along with transforming another 300 million low-resource-consuming peasants into perpetually consuming urbanites. As China's cities expand, as more cities are built, and more people move into urban areas, more energy is needed. In 1980, at the beginning of the economic boom period, China's installed energy capacity was 66 GW; by 2002 it was up to 350 GW; and now it's over 1,244 GW – a rate of growth that no country has never seen before. China already ranks as the number-one electricity producer in the world. By 2030 the country is expected to double its energy output yet again, adding an additional 1,500 GW of power. To give a sense of scale, the current total energy capacity of the USA is 1,052 GW. In the next two decades alone, China is expected to invest nearly $4 trillion in new power-generating operations as mass urbanization continues.

Coal

China's cities are powered by coal. Although the government claims to be trying to get away from this heavily polluting energy source, 78 per cent (758 GW) of China's electricity still comes from it. China uses almost as much coal as the rest of the world together. Despite the large scale of the public outcry over the atrocious air quality that causes over a million premature deaths per year, China is still in the process of expanding its coal power industry. The goal is to raise coal energy capacity by 75 per cent, tacking on another 557 GW from 363 new power plants, as the country's coal usage is expected to rise from 3.5 billion tons per year (2012) to 4.8 billion by 2020. Considering that each coal-fired power plant has a lifetime of between thirty and fifty years, smoggy skies are set to stay over China for the foreseeable future. Even though the country is making big strides in developing alternative energy sources, it shouldn't be presumed that China will derive less than 60 per cent of its energy capacity from coal at any point in the next decade.

The problems with China's coal dependency aren't restricted to air pollution either. The natural geology of the country has played a big trick on its contemporary residents, as the areas that are rich in coal tend to be deficient in water. Over 80 per cent of China's coal comes from areas where water supplies are considered by the United Nations to be at 'stressed' or 'absolute scarcity' levels. Some 60 per cent of China's coal power capacity is concentrated in six provinces, which account for just 5 per cent of the country's water. As all coal-fired power plants do is boil water in order to spin turbines with steam, a massive volume of water is needed to run and cool them – and that's without factoring in all the water needed in other phases of coal production. Depending on size and capacity, coal plants each withdraw between 70 and 180 billion gallons of water per year, with as much as 12 per cent lost to evaporation. Today, there are over 620 coal-fired power plants in China. The coal industry alone uses as much as 17 per cent of the country's water reserves. Coal power is sucking the aquifers of China's northern plains dry. According to a study by Beijing's Geological Environmental Monitoring Institute (GEMI), over-drawing of the shallow aquifer has pushed well-drillers into tapping the deep aquifer, which is non-replenishable. This doesn't bode well for a region where more than half of China's wheat and a third of its corn are grown. In heavily industrialized Hebei province, the level of the deep aquifer is receding by 3 metres per year, shrinking the amount of irrigated farmland, decreasing agricultural production, and causing subsidence, sinkholes and fissures – some of which is occurring in urban areas. The World Bank reported that 'Anecdotal evidence suggests that deep wells around Beijing now have to reach 1,000 meters to tap fresh water, adding dramatically to the cost of supply', and then predicted 'catastrophic consequences for future generations'.

The lack of water in the coal-rich north of China has resulted in a large-scale scheme that Mao Zedong once dreamed of. 'Southern water is plentiful, northern water scarce', he said. 'If at all possible, borrowing some water would be good.' And that's exactly what China is now doing with its US$62 billion dollar South–North Water Transfer Project. An estimated 44.8 billion cubic metres of water will be transferred each year from the Yangtze River and its tributaries in central China via three canal systems to feed the power plants, factories and ever-expanding cities of the north. The project was launched in 2002. In the beginning of 2014 the eastern most canal went into operation, carrying water from the Yangtze 1,467 km to factory-rich Shandong province. Later in the year the central route, which stretches from a tributary of the Yangtze 1,276 km to Beijing and Tianjin, was due to be put into operation. 'The project can be seen as emergency relief', Ma Jun, the director of the Institute of Public and Environmental Affairs in Beijing, told the *New York Times*. 'It's not a moment for celebration. There should be a sobering review of how we cornered ourselves so that we had to undertake a project with so much social and environmental impact' (Buckley 2013).

The South–North Water Transfer Project addresses the symptoms of one environmental problem while adding to another: water is not plentiful in the regions it is being taken from. In fact, Jiangxi province, on the Yangtze River, has been experiencing severe droughts over the past five years, and lakes and rivers in the region have been drying out as water has been diverted from them for other purposes, such as filling the reservoirs of the Three Gorges Dam. Water levels in the Han River, the Danjiangkou reservoir and Poyang lake have been prone to falling so low that local cities are regularly being hit by water shortages. Now, the volume of water required to supply California for six months is being taken out of this already water-deficient region each year to supply Beijing, Tianjin and Shandong province – a large price to pay to maintain the industrial status quo.

Hydropower

Large-scale hydraulic engineering has been a practice of the Chinese since the legendary Yu the Great was said to have invented dams over 4,000 years ago. The Dujiangyan Irrigation System, a levee which redirects a portion of the Min River through a mountain and into farmland, was built in 256 BCE, and is still functioning today. Through the ages the Chinese have built dams for flood control and irrigation, but in the twentieth and twenty-first centuries they have been built primarily for another reason: hydroelectricity. More than 22,000 dams over 15 metres high have been constructed across the country since 1950, and hundreds more are on the way.

Hydroelectric power is seen by China's political leaders as the most desirable alternative to coal, and it is easy to see why: dams are not thought of as a major source of air pollution; they provide renewable energy; China has more hydroelectric potential than any other country in the world; and dams are major construction projects which put large amounts of money into the pockets of the builders – which are all too often directly connected to various levels of government. Virtually all of China's dams are operated by a group of ten companies, which are mostly state-owned enterprises (SOEs), while dam construction tends to be undertaken by just three entities, which belong to the State Owned Assets Supervision and Administration Commission (SASAC) and the Chinese Armed Police Force. So the line between the companies profiting from dam building and the governments ordering their construction doesn't even have to be drawn: they are one and the same, a connection which has been dubbed China's 'hydro-industrial complex'.

Today, more than half the hydropower in the world is being generated in China. In 2015 the country is expected to be generating 325 GW of electricity from dams. By 2020 this figure is projected to be 430 GW – over 40 per cent of the current electrical capacity of the USA. China is adding an incredible 15 GW of hydropower per year. For comparison, only 1.9 GW of hydropower is generated in all of North America.

A hundred new dams are currently being built along the Yangtze River and its tributaries; twenty-four are going on the Lacang River (Mekong); while the Nu and Yarlung Tsangpo (Brahmaputra), the last of China's large free-flowing rivers, are to be dammed up along with the rest. These hydroelectric plants are often set up in series of a dozen, and sometimes two dozen or more, dams along a river in a row, creating a staircase of reservoirs. This turns sleek, fast-moving rivers into sluggish sequences of lakes, which resemble a string of beads when viewed from above. Apart from the obvious environmental impact of altering a river ecosystem so drastically, these dam cascades can have potentially catastrophic results if something goes wrong. If only one dam in the series bursts or even overflows, the deluge of excess water can cause a chain reaction of dams collapsing downstream. This has happened before. In 1975, the Banqiao dam on a tributary of the Huai River gave way in a massive rainstorm, which took down the other dams in the sequence, eventually producing a 7,300 sq km lake, which put six counties under water. An estimated 26,000 people died in the initial event and an additional 145,000 in the ensuing famine and epidemics.

Another issue with rampant dam development is that the best locations for hydroelectricity plants are often also areas of heightened seismic activity: dams are often erected in deep river valleys, which tend to share the same orientation as fault lines. The tremendous weight of the water stored in reservoirs, combined with the seasonal fluctuations in their water levels, creates additional pressure on these fault lines, and dams have duly been linked to earthquakes, as in the following example. The builders of the Zipingpu dam were warned by China's Earthquake Bureau of the potential danger in constructing the dam a little over a kilometre from a major fault, but they carried on with the project regardless. In May 2008 an earthquake of magnitude 7.9 struck Wenchuan, just 5.5 km away, killing 80,000 people. 'Since then, more than 50 studies have found evidence that the reservoir triggered small quakes through the fault system, culminating in the large quake' (Lewis 2013). Five years after this quake another – this time of magnitude 7.0 – occurred in Ya'an City on the same fault line, killing 200 people. According to the Sichuan Geology and Mineral Bureau, this event could have been an aftershock of the Wenchuan quake. China's continued dam building could prove to be a profoundly cataclysmic way of procuring energy for its cities, as a report by Probe International declared that 43 per cent of the 130 dams that China is in the process of building or is planning are located 'in zones of high to very high seismic hazard' (Jackson 2012).

Although hydroelectricity is conventionally thought of as a clean form of energy production, it is nevertheless the case that the reservoirs behind dams often become semi-stagnant lakes. Discharges from cities, factories and farms tend to find their way into the water systems – often being intentionally dumped there – 'creating a festering bog of effluent, silt, industrial pollutants and rubbish in the reservoir[s]' (InternationalRivers.org). This creates a major environmental hazard, as semi-stagnant reservoirs do not permit the passage of pollutants downstream as rivers do. Instead, they just sit there, often seeping into the aquifers below, rendering China's atrocious groundwater supply even more toxic. The problem of the build-up of pollution in reservoirs behind dams was revealed clearly in 2010 during a massive flood that brought the Three Gorges Dam to the brink of catastrophe. The dam was saved but a 50,000-square-metre mass of floating garbage sat congealed behind it, leading to a build-up so thick that the *Hubei Daily* claimed that 'people can literally walk on the water's surface'.

The construction of dams in China is also known for the massive social upheaval it causes. Over the past fifty years over 16 million people (more than the population of Ecuador) have been removed from their homes and relocated on account of hydroelectric development in China. The Three Gorges Dam alone flooded 13 cities, 140 towns and 1,350 villages, displacing 1.5 million people. 'With each new project, communities are fractured and lives disrupted. People are relocated to new towns or forced to resettle on degraded land. Often they do not receive promised resettlement money or job training, driving many to migrate again' (Lewis 2013).

Poyang Lake

I stood on the banks of what is China's largest freshwater lake, although it looked more like a mudflat. Fishing boats were laid out in uneven rows, flipped upside down on the moist soil. Around them grasses were growing and cows grazing. It was once all water. Kneeling down next to me was a fisherman who had given up the trade for the season; he was rearranging a bundle of steel scrap he had salvaged from the dried-up lake bed beyond. In the wet season, Poyang Lake is a gigantic 4,000 sq km expanse that stretches from the Yangtze River in the north to the city of Nanchang in the south. In the dry season it shrinks to a broad river, and in some places disappears entirely. Large seasonal fluctuations in water level are natural here; however, since the commissioning of the Three Gorges Dam, the world's largest hydroelectric system, these changes have been extreme. The reservoir for this dam reduces the water level of the Yangtze River; the deficit is partially made up for by pulling water out of Poyang Lake. In the dry season 6,000 cubic metres of water per second flow out of the lake, while only 1,000 cubic metres per second flow in, which makes the entire ecosystem retract and virtually dry out each year. To intensify the matter, Jiangxi province has been experiencing drought. Each year the dry season has been starting a little sooner; in consequence the water level drops lower, and the lake becomes smaller than it was the preceding year. In December 2014 Poyang Lake shrank to under

175 sq km – nearly twenty-three times smaller than it is during the wet season.

I walked along what was probably once a beautiful lakeside promenade. The walkway was stone-tiled and there were statues and large stone billboards with pictures, poems and stories carved into them. Today, the park has fallen into disrepair – it was built and then forgotten. A wooden pagoda that apparently once sat proudly upon a nearby hillock that jetted out into the lake bed had fallen into ruin. Its windows were broken, its doors were kicked in; candy wrappers, soda bottles, the remains of campfires, and human faeces with crumpled piles of toilet paper littered the floor. Not many people stroll down this way anymore, and there is a good reason for this: the lake is gone.

Poyang was once a main transport corridor between the Yangtze and Pearl River deltas, connecting commercially the central regions of China with the south. It was the site of one of the largest naval battles in history. Ancient poets wrote lines extolling its charms: 'Endless water merges into the floating cloud, / The immense lake looks boundless as it melts into the sky.' Now during each dry season this boundless lake becomes a mudflat. Poyang Lake is one of the last remaining refuges for an array of wildlife, much of which is rare or threatened. For instance, the nearly extinct finless porpoise is a resident here. Some 87 bird species overwinter at Poyang Lake, including eleven that are endangered. Over the past decade, though, their numbers have dropped tenfold. Less water means less food.

I continued walking along the dried-up lake bed and was soon standing below a temple that sat upon a 10-metre-high pedestal of earth. It's called Yinshan Island. However, it's not much of an island anymore as one can walk up to it. Cars now drive, children ride bicycles and livestock grazes where there was once a lake. Fishermen now have no fish to catch, so they stomp around in the mud, salvaging lost steel propellers and iron rudders to sell as scrap. Interestingly, the people I talked to here did not seem overly worried. Some still come down to the riverbank to photograph the mud or to gawk at the pedestal of land that they've always known to be an island. 'Next year there will be water', they told me confidently. 'The government will fix it.' Others cheered.

'It is like this every year', one man who grew up in Duchang told me.

'So the water went away like this when you were a kid?' I asked.

He thought for a moment and had a change of heart. 'No', he replied, 'it didn't. This year is worse than ever.'

Poyang is not alone in being drained by the Three Gorges. Dongting Lake in Hunan province has experienced extreme decreases in size, and myriad smaller lakes have completely vanished. The government of Jiangxi province has proposed a plan to preserve the lake by installing sluice gates at its mouth, reducing the outflow to the Yangtze River in the dry season. But this would only send the crisis further downstream – and downstream from here are Nanjing and Shanghai.

This is all on top of the fact that China's water-to-population ratio is always inadequate. The UN considers 1,700 cubic metres of fresh water per person to be 'stressed' provision. China is rapidly approaching the line, with just 1,730 cubic metres per person. The Ministry of Water Resources (MOWR) has declared that two-thirds of the cities in the country are running low on water. It estimates that by 2030 China's population will be consuming 750 billion cubic metres of water per year, which is about 90 per cent of the total available in the country. The Asian Development Bank, meanwhile, projects a bleaker vision: it predicts that the country's water demand may exceed its supply by 200 billion cubic metres.

The disappearance of bodies of water isn't an unusual phenomenon in contemporary China. According to the Ministry of Water Resources and the National Bureau of Statistics, China has lost 28,000 rivers since 1990 – half the rivers that once ran in the country. Hebei province, a major coal-producing region, once had 1,052 lakes. This number has dwindled to 83.

Not only is the Southeast Asia region in a battle with China for the rights to the water flowing along shared rivers, but within China itself an inter-province water war isn't beyond the realm of possibilities as each part of the country struggles to procure enough water to run its industries, power its cities, nurture its crops, and sustain its expanding urban population.

Other renewable energy sources

Although the coming decades will see China powered primarily by coal, the country is also rapidly developing non-fossil fuel – that is, renewable energy – sources. It is estimated that by 2020 some 700 GW – over 15 per cent – of China's energy capacity will be from non-fossil fuel sources, and it is predicted that by 2050 coal power will fall to between 30 and 50 per cent of the total energy supply.

Besides hydropower, China has been steadily building up its wind and solar industries, as well as beginning to develop biomass and geothermal energy sources. The numbers show that the country is serious about this endeavour; it's not simply an empty public relations exercise. Bloomberg New Energy Finance (BNEF) discovered that China's wind and solar sectors accrued US$68 billion in investments in 2012 alone. China has the greatest potential for wind energy production on the planet, estimated at 2,380 GW of exploitable capacity on land and another 200 GW offshore, where three-quarters of the country's wind farms are currently located. In 2010, China duly became the largest producer of wind energy in the world. By the end of 2012 its wind turbines were generating 76 GW of electricity nationwide. Not satisfied with this, China aims to increase its wind power capacity to 100 GW by 2020.

China broke a record by installing an incredible 12 GW of solar power in 2013 – three times the UK's current solar capacity – bringing its total up to nearly 20 GW. China's National Development and Reform Commission aims to establish this incredible growth as a trend, adding 10 GW of solar power each year to meet the 100 GW goal by 2020. For a sense of scale, the entire solar energy capacity of the planet is currently 140 GW. In addition, off-grid methods of utilizing solar energy, such as for heating water, are also ubiquitous throughout the country.

The law of diminishing returns

Air, water and earth are being despoiled as China moves forward with its urbanization movement. The atrocious air quality in most parts of the country hardly needs to be mentioned here. Air pollution is no longer localized to big cities and industrial zones; it has become so bad that expanses of smog thick enough to shut down entire cities can now stretch across multiple provinces. Some 50 per cent of China's water is below international standards for drinkable water; 40 per cent of the country's rivers are rated as seriously polluted, with 20 per cent being too toxic to even come into contact with (Jiang 2008). Some 20 to 40 per cent of China's arable soil is known to be contaminated, and an estimated 13 million tons of crops harvested each year are laced with heavy metals (Wong 2013). When the law of diminishing returns kicks in, whereby decades of rampant pollution demand regular large-scale and very expensive clean-up procedures, a major drain on the profits of urbanization may soon come to pass. Along with this will come rising health-care costs and ever-increasing social discontent from a population that is literally dying for economic progress. China seems to view nature as something to conquer. This process has placed trophies on the shelf of human achievement, but it has also left behind very extensive wastelands. The toll of China's urbanization movement is currently being paid for by the country's environment. This is one debt that even the Communist Party may not be able to wipe off the books.

EIGHT

The unsinkable ship

'You are rich? You don't even have your house! So maybe you're not that rich.'

Cities make money. The more cities there are, the more money is made – or at least that is the thinking. Most business takes place in urban areas; that is where most GDP is created, where economies are built and destroyed. The McKinsey Institute predicts that 'growing cities could inject up to $30 trillion a year into the world economy by 2025'. It also estimates that by the same year just 600 cities worldwide will be generating 65 per cent of global economic growth. The world's economic centre of gravity is shifting ever eastwards, and China is now at its heart. Of the 75 cities that the McKinsey Institute predicts will be the most economically dynamic by 2025, 29 are in China. Their average rate of growth is an incredible 365 per cent, dwarfing all of the other cities on the list. When the backhoes are digging, when the cement trucks are pouring, when cranes are lifting, money is being spent and money is being made.

Urbanization is a financial movement; each new city, district and town is an investment. China is redrawing its map and re-structuring its society, but what is the cost of this investment? According to China's Ministry of Finance, the projected price tag for the Xi administration's 'National New-type Urbanization Plan', which covers urbanization efforts from 2014 to 2020, is US$6.8 trillion. By 2030, the much-fabled year when China is expected to have a billion people in its cities, the country expects its current US$9.4 trillion per year GDP to have more than quadrupled, surpassing that of the USA twice over. Much of this projected future growth is calculated on the basis of today's ongoing urbanization movement. What the new catalysts of commerce become will define the role the country will play in the future and may well be the factor that determines whether the rise of China tops out and flourishes or goes bust.

The housing bubble

Over 2 billion square metres of new floor space is created each year as China's housing capacity grows by an incredible 13.4 per cent annually. It seems that China can't build houses fast enough; prices keep rising as the people keep buying. But how long can this last?

When Ye Qiu told me that she had bought another property, I had to suppress my surprise. All I could do was ask how. I knew she wasn't exactly reeling in the money with her unlicensed tutoring service. In the best months she and her fiancé together make only around RMB20,000 (roughly US$3,200). While this is a decent living wage in China, it hardly seems enough to finance the buying of homes that aren't really needed – in Ye Qiu's case, two new homes that she won't be using any time soon.

Two types of housing are available in China: *baozhang xingzhu fang*, 'economically affordable houses', and *shangpin fang*, commodity houses. Economically affordable houses are subsidized by the government; developers get breaks on land prices and receive tax credits; and the final products are sold at just 3–5 per cent over the cost of production. There are strict regulations concerning the purchase and sale of this type of property: it is only for families with low to medium incomes who have under a set amount in net assets and a local living permit (*hukou*); the owner must actually live in the house; the property must not be resold within five years of purchase; and if it was acquired with a mortgage, this must be fully paid off before resale. Such houses are meant for residents, not investors. There is a major qualification, however: while economically affordable housing costs significantly less than commodity houses, the properties are still not exactly *economical*, and tend to be out of the financial reach of most people. Furthermore, they are not that plentiful, making up just 3 per cent of housing being built – notably, at the end of the 1990s the figure was 25 per cent. Although according to the new urbanization plan announced in March 2014, the total amount of economically affordable housing should soon rise to 23 per cent nationwide.

Commodity houses, on the other hand, are free-market properties that can be bought and sold at will; prices are not capped by the government, and restrictions on ownership are more lax. When people discuss the Chinese 'housing bubble' they are mostly referring to the country's commodity housing market.

Although it varies greatly in different parts of China, the cost of an apartment is high everywhere. According to the IMF's house price-to-wage ratio, China's big cities are, relatively speaking, some of the most expensive in the world in which to buy real estate. This ratio measures median housing prices in a city in relation to median disposable income to calculate the minimum amount of time it would take for an average resident to pay for a property.

According to this evaluation method, China, including Hong Kong, has seven out of the world's top ten most expensive cities for residential property. In Beijing, it would take 22.3 years to buy a property, in Shanghai 15.9 years, in Tianjin 10.3 years, and in Chongqing 6.3 years. This means that, relatively to salary, Beijing's housing prices are twice as high as in Tokyo, three times higher than in London, and four times higher than in New York City.

High housing prices in China were a sudden development, relatively speaking. Fifteen years ago property developers didn't even exist. Prior to 1988 land transactions were not permitted and all property outside of a few SEZs was fully owned and operated by the government. It wasn't until the mid-1990s that home privatization policies began, which enabled the Chinese to buy and sell real estate for the first time. During the transition people were given the option to purchase the home they were living in at a very low rate. But by 1998, the private housing market had exploded, private developers began appearing, and a storm of industries arose that would shape, drive and define the domestic economy and fiscal system of China as the country matures through the reform period. China rarely does things halfway, and so by 2010 its property market was already the largest in the world.

As could be expected, prices surged. From 2005 to 2009 the cost of real estate in China tripled. According to Nomura, in the big four cities – Beijing, Guangzhou, Shenzhen and Shanghai – home prices increased by 20–25 per cent in 2013 alone. A clear example of this can be found in Daxing, a suburb an hour by metro south of Beijing. In 2010, apartments there sold for RMB11,000 per square metre; by 2013 the price had more than doubled to RMB23,000 per square metre. In the Wudaokou part of the city, where Tsinghua and Peking universities are located, the cost of housing rose by a factor of twenty-five, from RMB4,000 to over RMB100,000 per square metre, between 2000 and 2013. Although Beijing has the highest housing prices in the country, the overall trend is more or less the same nationwide: the average cost of residential property in China is getting more and more expensive. The fear of perpetually rising real-estate prices has become a self-fulfilling prophecy, as consumer sentiments such as 'The price keeps going up. If I don't buy a house now I will never be able to afford one' and 'It's not possible to wait, as the longer you wait the higher prices go' have become commonplace throughout Chinese society.

Even though residential apartments are incredibly expensive, the Chinese covet property nonetheless. They love talking about property, reading about property, shopping for property and, especially, buying property. In 2012 alone people in China spent over US$1 trillion on real estate. The Chinese general public speak of fluctuations in housing prices with the zeal of Americans discussing the latest football scores. Everybody knows how expensive real estate is; nevertheless, owning a house – or, in some cases, many houses – is as invigorating as ever. 'A house is not just a house; it means a lot', Ye Qiu explained to me.

> A house gives you Face. Houses are the main subject of conversation now. 'Did you buy a house? Where is your house? How big is your house? How many extra houses do you have?' people always ask each other. My sister told me that at her class reunion this year most of her classmates have their own house; they were talking about them; but some of her classmates who didn't have a house yet just sat there and kept silent. They don't have a common topic with those who have houses.

The quality of an individual's real-estate holdings is now the main indicator of status, and the dividing line between the haves, the have-nots and the trying-to-haves.

Whereas the Chinese housing market may look like a bubble, the demand for property is real. There is a lot of pressure on young couples to own a home prior to getting married. Also a young man who does not own an apartment generally fares less well in finding an appropriate mate in a country with 30 million more males than females. 'No house, no wife', a young man desperately searching for a home in Shanghai once told me. In a society where parents are generally supported by their children in old age, finding adequate marriage partners for their children is akin to a social security plan. This puts enormous pressure on families to gather the resources to enable their children to enter into profitable marriages and settled in homes of their own. As there are some 13 million weddings in China each year, and newlyweds account for fully one-third of residential property sales, this cultural aspect alone continuously invigorates the housing market (Rothman 2014). Add to this the further demand that comes from a society that is growing richer and, accordingly, seeks to move up the property ladder. Then there is the fact that China's urban population is predicted to increase by 26 per cent in the next ten years, adding 21 million more people each year. All in all the demand for housing is extreme – and this is without addressing the issue of real-estate speculation and the investment mania that has sprung up around residential property.

Ye Qiu told me that her sister owns three houses.

> She said, 'If you work in a city for many years, when you quit the job and leave the city you might think, what do you have after working those years? If you have your own house, you can say that's what I have.' She also said that no matter how long you work in a city, if you don't have a house there you have no sense of belonging; you can't call it your home.

This is the prevailing attitude throughout the country. Home ownership – not renting, leasing or sharing – is what's of the essence. To this end, partly, China has one of the highest home ownership rates in the world.

The Chinese housing market is more akin to a tourist trap than a bubble. Tourist towns are overpriced because vendors know that customers have money and no other place to spend it. The same goes for housing in China: there is a more or less captive consumer base; by limiting the investment options, people's money can be funnelled into real estate. China's bank interest rates don't keep up with inflation, the domestic stock market is extremely risky and there are few other viable financial options for storing savings or investing money. Notwithstanding the considerable media attention the so-called 'housing bubble' has been getting lately both in China and abroad, the faith that the Chinese have in the value of housing is still virtually unflappable. This isn't necessarily because they aren't aware that the market could fall out from under them, but because they feel that it is still the best option available to them.

The new Chinese currency

Think of apartments in China as blocks of gold. Just as one doesn't have to mould a piece of gold into something functional like a piece of jewellery for it to have value, so one doesn't need to live in an apartment in China for it to have worth. Just as gold will always be valuable in a world that wants it, there will always be demand for housing in a country of 1.4 billion people. This demand will only be strengthened by the 300 million-plus more people who are expected to migrate to urban areas by 2030.

Houses in China are ways of quantifying and qualifying value, and have become a tradable commodity that is invested in very much like stocks or bonds.

Houses are likewise the ultimate touchstone of status. The quantity, value and location of the real estate that someone owns is taken as a direct indication of their success and standing. So the Chinese scamper to collect multiple apartments they never have any intention of actually using. According to Nomura, 21 per cent of China's urban households possess more than one home. The chimes of China's housing market ring even louder as the country reshuffles the socio-economic layouts of its cities and pushes the trendy/downtown areas out to the new districts, which just happens to be where most of the newly available luxury housing stock is located, thus creating a feeding frenzy of investors wanting to get in early, buy low and sell high – or to hide illicitly obtained wealth.

Affording expensive homes – house slaves and the moonlight clan

'But how do people here afford to pay for their houses? How did *you* pay for your houses?' I asked Ye Qiu. Throughout China I have met low-level white-collar workers who have been able to purchase homes in the overinflated Chinese real-estate market on salaries that shouldn't come close to being able to fund them.

'Most of the young people, of course, don't make so much money by themselves, so they ask their parents for help', Ye Qiu explained.

'Some rich parents help their children pay the full price. Some are not so rich, so they help their children make the downpayment, and leave them to pay the monthly mortgage themselves. Some are poor; they can't help their children buy a house, but they can help them by borrowing money from others.'

'Did your parents help you buy your house?'

'Well, we paid RMB120,000 for the downpayment. My father gave us RMB20,000, my sister lent us RMB40,000, we borrowed RMB20,000 from our friends, and the rest was our savings.'

Ye Qiu bought her first house a year after she graduated from university in Huizhou, Guangdong province, which is near to Guangzhou, where she is originally from. At RMB4,100 per square metre, the three-bedroom, 97-square-metre pad cost her nearly RMB400,000 (US$65,000), which she said was a good deal for the area. That was in 2013. The value of the property has already jumped past RMB500,000.

Fuelled by the thought of making RMB100,000 profit in such a short time, Ye Qiu set out to buy a second home as an investment. She found a 47.9-square-metre one-bedroom place in the centre of Huizhou near the government building for RMB6,000 per square metre. Buying this second property required a little more ingenuity than the first. She and her boyfriend, of course, did not have the RMB287,400 needed to purchase the property outright, so they had to find an alternative financing strategy.

First they put off their marriage. One tactic the Chinese government claims to be trying in order to cool down the housing market is to regulate the amount of financing people can receive to purchase property. A first property requires a 30 per cent downpayment; the second needs 60 per cent; any additional house beyond this must be paid for in full upfront, with no financing allowed. Additionally, if a multiple homeowner wishes to resell one of their properties they are hit by an additional 20 per cent property tax – which, with current housing prices, can amount to hundreds of thousands of RMB. Not able to make the huge downpayment on their second home, Ye Qiu and her boyfriend chose a popular loophole: not getting married. So one house would be in his name and the other in hers. This is not uncommon: many Chinese are choosing to postpone marriage or even getting divorced in order to benefit financially in their dealings with real estate. Indeed, right after these new regulations went into effect China saw its divorce rate spike by 45 per cent. 'We have to say that the house is changing our Chinese lives!' Ye Qiu exclaimed.

After postponing their wedding, Ye Qiu and her husband-to-be needed to procure a little over RMB86,000 for the downpayment and the bank would take care of the rest. They amassed their savings and put the word out to their friends, who contributed the additional funds. They then took out a bank loan for RMB200,000 at 6.2 per cent interest and bought the new apartment. The standards for qualifying for a home mortgage in China are relatively low. Generally speaking, a borrower's monthly salary must be at least twice the monthly payment, and that's about it.

I asked Ye Qiu how she pays her mortgages out with their relatively modest income. She explained that she had already paid off the debt from her first house, so all she has to worry about now is the second one.

> First, we have to pay the mortgage: it's RMB5,000 a month. Second, we have a car, the cost for fuel and maintenance is around RMB1,000 a month. Third, food costs some RMB1,000 a month. Clothes and having fun are not fixed expenditures. Because I borrowed some money from my friends, I now spend less on clothes and pleasure; after we have paid off the debt we will spend more money on fun.

The rest of her income goes towards savings.

Ye Qiu then gave me a run-down of how some of her friends manage to pay for their homes:

> Julong has worked in the telecommunications office in his hometown since he graduated from college. He earns RMB4,000 a month. Last year he bought a house in the town. He made the downpayment with his parents' help and borrowed some money from his friends. His monthly mortgage payment is RMB2,000. And he has to pay back the borrowed money. He also has to save to decorate the house, because the houses in China mostly are *maopeifang*, rough-cast [empty, bare concrete-walled cavities].
>
> Guichen is a friend from my university. He became a civil servant after he graduated. He earns RMB3,000 a month. He bought a house in our hometown last year. The house was cheaper than those in town because it is specially for civil servants. His parents helped him with the downpayment. His monthly mortgage payment is RMB1,200.
>
> Xiaofeng is a traffic policeman in Guangzhou. He earns RMB8,000 a month. He bought a house last year. He borrowed some money from his relatives and friends for the downpayment. His mortgage is RMB5,000 a month. The house he bought cost him RMB8,000 per square metre, though houses in the area are usually above RMB15,000 per square metre. Why was the house he bought cheaper for him? Because it was built specially for civil servants.

'From these we can see that almost every friend of mine spends most of his or her salary on houses', she confirmed. 'That tells us a lot: everyone wants a house; whether he or she is rich or not, whether they have the money themselves or borrow from their friends or relatives, they will buy a house.'

This has led to an entire sector of Chinese society becoming known as *fangnu*: house slaves. These are homeowners who are almost completely financially strapped to their property, often allocating in excess of 70 per cent of their disposable income to their mortgages. Because they must dedicate such a large portion of their income to their house, what they can do socially or for leisure is severely limited, and their day-to-day quality of life duly suffers. Ye Qiu and the new homeowners she cited spend between 25 and 62.5 per cent of their total income on their mortgages, which is in line with the national average of 30–50 per cent. They own their own homes but live hand to mouth as a consequence. But this is seen as preferable to the alternative.

'Those of my friends who don't buy a house – it's not because they don't want to or think there's a bubble in the housing market, it's because they don't have money!' Ye Qiu exclaimed. Oddly, it's this lack of money that often leads to less indiscriminate spending and an all-round better day-to-day quality of life. As Ye Qiu explained:

> Yanqing works in a foreign-language institution in Huizhou. She teaches South Koreans Chinese. She earns RMB3,500 a month. She flat-shares with her friend; the rent for each is RMB500 a month. The cost of living for her is RMB800–1,000 a month, including food, transport, telephone and Internet. She sends home RMB500 per month. She spends the rest of her money on entertainment, having dinner with friends and buying clothes and so on. I asked her how much money she saves in a month. She told me that she has almost no savings! I asked why she didn't save money. She said, 'There's no impetus for me to save money. The price of housing is so high, there's no way I can buy a house by saving. I can just give myself a better life now.' What about the future? 'I don't know. Maybe I will marry a rich man; then I can become rich too and have my own house.' She has worked for two and a half years since graduating from college; she has almost no savings.

Yanqing is what has come to be known as *yue guang zu*: the moonlight clan. In Mandarin, the term 'moonlight' is a near homophone with the phrase for 'spend all your monthly salary' and has been applied typically to young people who spend their excess money rather than saving it. Acquiring enough money to buy a house often feels like a futile endeavour for many of China's young adults who don't make enough money or have the financial support networks to lend it to them. Oftentimes, they're right. If one is making only US$500 per month and dropping half of this on living expenses it's going to be a very long time before one will be able to afford a home in China's expensive property market. So, faced with a seemingly unsurmountable financial barrier, many find little incentive to save; they therefore give up, spending their disposable income freely and enjoying themselves. While the moonlight clan brashly break from the Chinese tradition of saving a large portion of their income, the barriers they face to home ownership and financial solvency are far greater than preceding generations of Chinese have faced. This leaves an entire population of young adults suspended in socio-economic stagnancy and hopelessness, and so many quit chasing a Chinese Dream that is galloping too far ahead for them to catch up.

In China's big vibrant cities and provincial capitals affordable housing for the middle and working classes is often very difficult to find. The hostels of the country's tier-one cities are full of guests who have made themselves permanent fixtures in dormitories because they simply cannot find a home they can afford. They go to work during the day just to return to the almost futile search for a home at night. All the while, tens of millions of homes sit empty across the country and hundreds of thousands more are being built each year that most of the society cannot afford. This discrepancy isn't just having a dire social and economic impact on society; it is also a health risk. The Chinese Medical Doctors Association has found that buying a house is the biggest cause of stress among China's white-collar population.

One of China's biggest hurdles is building the type of housing that is needed, where it is needed. Available apartments are everywhere in China, but unfortunately they're often priced too high for those who actually want to live in them. There are over 400 million middle- and upper-class people in China – more than the total population of the USA – and developers are cashing in on this social ascension by building more and more luxury housing developments, potentially pushing this type of property far into the realm of oversupply. The logic here is simple: higher-class homes can be sold for more money; as developers often pay top price for residential construction land, they want to squeeze as much revenue as possible out of each square metre. It has been predicted that China will need to provide 10 million new homes per year to provide for incoming rural migrants alone – and this needs to be the affordable kind of housing. China will have to act fast if it is to make good on its current urbanization ambitions.

Even though housing in China tends to be expensive and huge numbers of young adults are searching in vain, most Chinese are amazingly able to eventually procure a home for themselves. According to Beijing's National Bureau of Statistics (NBS), the homeownership rate in China is 80 per cent. This is partially due to the way that the home privatization process began. Faced with the task of transferring public-owned housing to the private sector, the central government devised a programme called the Housing Provident Fund. This fund, which is similar to the USA's 401(k) plan, created an employer-matched savings system, which was combined with artificially low real-estate prices- and subsidized mortgage rates to assist people in buying a home. The employer-matched savings aspect of this programme is still in operation; it is one of the ways that the Chinese are able to pull together the massive amounts of money that it takes to own a roof over their heads. The explosion in home mortgages is a relatively recent development, which proliferated proportionate to the astronomical rise in housing cost and the creation of an open lending environment. Yet, when compared with other countries, China's reliance on home mortgages appears minuscule. Only 18 per cent of Chinese households have mortgages, compared with 49 per cent in the USA; and China's home mortgage-to-GDP ratio was just 15 per cent in 2012, whereas in the USA it was an incredible 81.4 per cent. As far as the house slaves with big mortgages go, very few will ever default on their loans. According to China Construction Bank, the bad-loan rate in the home-mortgage sector is a mere 0.2 per cent.

Notwithstanding the added expenditures and rising housing costs that the Chinese are now experiencing, many are making enough money still to be able to save. Nominal income growth in urban China has recently been rising 13 per cent each year, which, though not a direct correlation, clearly outpaces the 9 per cent average annual rise in housing costs over the past eight years up to 2014 (Rothman 2014). Per-capita disposable income in China has now risen to RMB26,955 per year, up from RMB9,421 in 2005, while the country's savings rate is the second highest in the world. The Chinese are able to afford their homes, even though they are extremely expensive.

Controlling the fire

On the question of whether it is a bubble, it should be noted that China's colossal market in real-estate speculation is more financially isolated than it seems. Although real-estate investment is rampant, investors are paying with cash – especially now that financing streams are being tightened up. According to Centaline Property Agency, homebuyers in expensive cities like Shanghai, Beijing and Guangzhou pay on average 50 per cent of an apartment's price up front. Nationwide, some 15 per cent of residential property is paid for in full with cash upfront. This means that a drop in the housing market does not necessarily involve mass banking defaults and a resulting chain reaction rippling through the entire economy. For this reason, the so-called housing bubble in China cannot be compared with that of the USA in 2008. As David Semple, director of International Equity at Van Eck Global, told *Forbes*: 'There is still very low leverage per capita in China. In the US, homeowners were over-leveraged and so when their housing prices declined they had no real source of capital anymore. China is not Dubai on steroids. You don't buy with no money down there' (Rapoza 2014). If you want to deal in property in China you bring cash to the table.

With real-estate prices in China as high as they currently are now, letting some air out of the 'bubble' may not be a bad thing. In the case of new cities with large numbers of high-priced commodity housing, a price drop seems inevitable if they are to attract enough residents to become fully functioning urban centres. This is exactly what we were seeing at the mid-point of 2014. According to China's NBS, across the country the cost of real estate is beginning to top out. At the beginning of the year prices were rising by 9 per cent per month but then began dropping rapidly. By September they were down to a mere 0.5 per cent increase per month, as the top of the bell curve seemed to have been reached. This fluctuation is not accounted for purely by market forces, however.

The degree to which the various levels of government in China control the property market should not be underestimated. Central and local governments know how to funnel massive numbers of consumers into the housing market; how to create, adapt or revoke policies to manipulate the cost of housing; and, by extension, how to make real estate a financially very dynamic industry. It has to be remembered that land sales are what keep the wheels of municipalities throughout China spinning; real-estate development is directly downstream from this. As residential property is taxed only on the initial sale – in contrast to commercial or industrial properties, which continuously add tax revenue to government coffers – local municipalities squeeze the amount of residential construction land they make available in order to keep the price they can get for it as high as possible. 'The starting point of local governments is to keep land prices relatively high. Governments are not willing to see home prices fall', the deputy chief of the China Land Surveying and Planning Institute told Reuters (Shao and Qing 2013). The initial price at which the government sells construction land to developers will reverberate through the entire sale process. As a general rule, what developers pay for a parcel of land will account for 50 per cent of the final sale price. In cities all over China local governments have been raising and raising the price of residential construction land. This is a reaction both to the eventuality that they will one day run out of land to sell and to simple market forces: residential development land is in high demand. The cost of housing rises proportionately with the cost of land. 'A rising tide lifts all boats' (Shao and Qing 2013).

The fact is that an overinflated housing market is one of the biggest cash cows the Communist Party has, and so the last thing they want is plummeting prices. 'With one hand on a patchwork of controls aimed at taming record house prices, governments with their other hand are at the same time selling land to developers at rising prices' (Shao and Qing 2013). 'On the one hand, the government introduced many policies to bring down the housing price; on the other they are driving price increases', Ye Qiu explained. 'There are a variety of housing related taxes, such as value-added real estate tax, land value-added tax, real estate transaction tax, property tax, property transfer tax, education tax, and so on.' Taxes and fees can be up to 60 per cent of a house's final price. To discover the source of the rocketing Chinese real-estate market one needs to look no further than the government.

China's real estate market has been marked by successive waves of booms followed by intentionally triggered cooling-off periods. According to the Milken Institute, these tidal fluctuations ebb and flow roughly every two years. That is, property prices in China spike then fall, spike then fall; this can be represented as a series of bell curves lined up side by side (Milken Institute 2012).

When attempting to critique the Chinese housing market one simple, keystone fact needs to be kept in mind: the Communist Party is in control. Both central and local government in China know how to manipulate their respective markets, directly controlling supply and manipulating demand by concocting favourable or unfavourable policies for the consumer while dictating how and where they can invest their money.

There is a very good reason for this excessive degree of governmental involvement: real-estate and related industries are responsible for 16 to 25 per cent of total GDP, 33 per cent of fixed asset investment, 10 per cent of urban employment, 15 per cent of bank loans, and they fuel forty other industries in China. In point, the building, development and sale of real estate forms an extremely important pillar of the country's economy, which isn't going to be left to the whims of the free market.

Too big to fail

Urbanization is a very expensive investment, especially at the scale and pace at which China is generating it. The official estimated price tag for urbanizing an additional 100 million people by 2020 is US$6–8 trillion – on top of the money the country has already spent on urbanizing, of course. As China's cities continue expanding with new districts, cities, towns and CBDs, they are also piling on the debt. As we've seen, China's fiscal system is fundamentally imbalanced. It leaves municipalities to depend on land sales and other business endeavours to fill their coffers and fund their development initiatives. This has put many local municipalities heavily into debt. China's National Audit Office estimated that by June 2013 local government debt had grown to US$3.3 trillion – more than the total GDP of France.

It's interesting to note here that since 1994 China's local governments have been prohibited from taking out loans. If that's the case, then how is it that they owe so much money? As with most bureaucratic regulations in China, there are loopholes. Rather than borrowing money directly from lenders, municipalities set up a separate company called a local government financing vehicle (LGFV), and that company takes out the loans and funnels the money to the city. So when Shanghai wanted to create Nanhui New City, it first set up a company called Lingang New Harbor City to borrow the required funds. The borrower and the city are of course one and the same, and the debt that is racked up is the responsibility of the municipality. There are now some 6,000 LGFVs in China, which between them have racked up nearly 15 per cent of the country's total outstanding loans. On paper this looks like impending disaster, a country full of Detroits that are fated to send the entire country into a downward spiral of financial despair, but in reality it's a little different. Wuhan, Wenzhou, Dongguang, Yujiapu and Ordos have all more or less gone bankrupt in recent years. However, a caveat built into China's fiscal system says that cities are not allowed to fail. So no city in modern China will ever file for bankruptcy. Indeed the term 'government bankruptcy' doesn't exist in the Chinese lexicon. So when Wuhan, soon to be a megacity in the heart of the country, reported US$33 billion of debt – twice its GDP and far larger than Detroit's – it wasn't the crisis it otherwise may seem. The same went for Ordos when it disclosed a debt exceeding US$50 billion, when its yearly revenue is just US$13 billion; and for Tianjin, which borrowed half its annual GDP to build the Yujiapu CBD without a plan for how it was going to pay it back.

This is because the Chinese financial system is a little different from that of most other countries. When considering domestic 'debt' in China, what we're really discussing is the amount of money the Communist Party owes to the Communist Party. 'What we have in China is a Communist Party-controlled bank lending money to a Communist Party-controlled local government to build Communist Party-approved public infrastructure', Andy Rothman, an economist for the Shanghai-based brokerage firm CLSA, told NPR (Langfitt 2014). So, as this is a matter of the various appendages of the same organization transferring money between each other, such terms as 'default' and 'bankruptcy' don't have the same ominous ring as they would if the money was being moved between contending entities which would demand payment in full. When a city in China gets into financial difficulties Beijing is always right there to rebalance the ledger books.

To echo what a financial strategist in Nanhui New City had told me would happen in the event of a crash, 'The government will take care of it. The government will lose a lot of money but we will be fine.'

In addition to Chinese municipalities, Chinese companies get bailed out too. When Suntech Power defaulted on a US$541 million debt, the city of Wuxi, where the company is based, was right there to provide the money required to save it. When China Credit Equals Gold, a trust fund managed by the Industrial and Commercial Bank of China (ICBC), needed a half-billion-dollar bail-out, the Chinese government fronted the bill. In 2014, Zhejiang Xingrun Real Estate Company claimed to be unable to pay its US$400 million debt, and so the central government stepped in and made it go away. Since 1998 Chinese banks have wiped more than US$3 trillion of corporate debt off the books. This process of bailing out companies that ultimately serve the broader ambitions of the state – or are owned by the state – has been going on for a long time in modern China. In the 1990s Shanghai instructed its banks to roll over the loans that the struggling developers who built the Pudong CBD owed. Basically, state-owned enterprises borrowing money from state-owned banks is just a formal front for the Communist Party spending its own money for its own ends. This is attested to by the fact that a huge majority of loans coming from Chinese banks (85 per cent in 2009) are going to SOEs, even though these state-owned companies amount to only 3.1 per cent of the total enterprises in the country.

What critics of China's local debt seem to miss is that the money that municipalities and developers are borrowing is not being squandered; it is pumped directly into the economic system – in one way or another. The money goes to developers, construction companies, architecture firms, funnelled through related industries, and into the pockets of labourers.

China's urbanization movement could be touted as the greatest economic stimulus plan in history. With explicit stimulus, such as 2008's US$586 billion and 2015's US$1.1 trillion plans, and implicit stimulus in the form of loans to municipalities and subsequent bailouts, the central government is injecting massive amounts of money into urban development. This is especially pertinent when we realize that nearly two dozen of China's big industries are in a continual state of oversupply, with many surviving off subsidies. China needs something to do with its excess of steel, concrete and coal, and building new infrastructure is currently part of the de facto solution. At this point, sustaining the country politically, economically and socially means pumping it with cash. China is a world in and of itself, and it has an economy that plays by its own rules.

The New South China Mall

The New South China Mall is in Dongguan, a city in the Pearl River Delta, an area known as the 'world's factory'. It was here that a local named Alex Hu built an instant-noodle empire. Becoming extremely wealthy, he decided to monumentalize his country's rags-to-riches story by building the largest shopping mall the world has ever known. As one of the first big shopping malls in the country it was intended to usher in a new age of domestic consumerism and show the world that a communist country could also have the world's greatest shrine to capitalism. The *New York Times* called it 'proof of China's new consumer culture'. *Newsweek* called it one of the seven 'new wonders of the world'. Researchers were sent to malls all over the world to gather ideas. They returned with a bag of tricks intended to make the place the mother of all shopping complexes. Sections were created to look like Amsterdam, Paris, Rome, Venice, Egypt, the Caribbean and California, each boasting the architecture, facades and monuments of the places they showcased, including an 82-foot replica of the Arc de Triomphe, a copy of Venice's St Mark's bell tower, and a giant Egyptian sphinx. They also built their own 2.1 km canal transportation network, in which gondolas would transport shoppers from wing to wing of this massive mall. An amusement park, which contained a 553 metre indoor–outdoor roller coaster, and one of the biggest IMAX cinemas in the country were added.

When construction was completed in 2005 the noodle man's masterpiece covered more than 9.5 million square feet and had 2,350 retail spaces. It became the largest mall on the planet, dwarfing the Edmonton Mall as well as the Mall of America, which is only half its size. Some 70,000 shoppers per day were expected to flood into this icon of the New China. However, nobody showed up. Ironically, very few retailers ever signed up to be a part of the greatest retail venture the world has ever known, and when the New South China Mall opened for business its stores were 99 per cent unoccupied. The place never had a chance to die; for it wasn't born to begin with. Nine years later this hasn't really changed.

The reason behind the initial stagnancy of the mall was simple: the location was horrible. Alex Hu wanted to build this masterpiece for his home city, but he didn't seem to take into account the fact that it is mostly made up of factories and the population is mostly rural migrant manual labourers – definitely not the target clientele for a high-end shopping mall. Although it is not too far from Shenzhen, Hong Kong and Guangzhou, there are no efficient transportation arteries to enable people to get there. The mall was built in the middle of nowhere, hence unable to attract pedestrian shoppers and difficult even for

Dongguan residents to access. It took me over two hours to get there on a city bus from Dongguan's main train station, which drove me through factory towns, fallow farms, rows of car repair shops, noodle joints, cigarette kiosks, soot-laden apartment blocks, and expanses of churned up, empty lots awaiting construction crews.

The New South China Mall should have fallen into bankruptcy long ago, but because it is such a massive and well-publicized project it was 'too big to fail'. An investment arm of Beijing University eventually bought out the project. Perhaps in an effort to save the mall – or to save face – the immediate surroundings are being built up with new high-rises; so perhaps at some point a captive consumer base can be manufactured and the New South China Mall become a monument to the somewhat irrational resolve that China is willing to put into its large-scale projects. Nobody is calling it quits yet.

Even though the scale of China's bad corporate debt is huge, lenders continue to make money. Even as banks expunged US$3.5 billion of debt in the first half of 2013, they nevertheless made US$76 billion, which set a record. Meanwhile Industrial and Commercial Bank of China (ICBC), the richest bank in the world, earned US$42.3 billion in profit in 2013, a 10.2 per cent increase over the year before.

The reason why these bailouts don't result in financial disaster – or often even a hiccup – is because Chinese banks are prepared for such things in the form of a massive reserve of liquid funds set aside in the event of large-scale default. As of June 2013 China's five largest banks had stockpiled 272 per cent of the value of their bad debt. The Chinese government mandates its banks to maintain a reserve requirement ratio (RRR) of 20 per cent, which means that a full fifth of a bank's deposits must be kept in reserves and not lent out, a protective measure against defaults. Internationally speaking, China's reserve requirement is very high, as the USA only demands that its big banks hold back a minimum of 10 per cent. Canada, the UK, Australia and Sweden don't even have an RRR. For this reason China's banking system is vastly more conservative and secure than that of many other countries. On top of this, China's banks are funded primarily by deposits rather than loans, as is the case with those in the USA, and are therefore 'less vulnerable to a liquidity crunch' (Milken Institute 2012).

The bulk of China's debt is domestic, meaning that it's simply money owed to the big four banks of the Communist Party; the chances of these creditors demanding repayment and causing mass default is low. Although many critics decry the fact that China has racked up a large amount of foreign debt, approximately US$1 trillion at the time of writing, it actually amounts to only 4 per cent of its total credit and roughly 10 per cent of its GDP. 'Debt really only becomes a problem when you need to go outside for financing. China doesn't depend on foreigners to finance itself' (Rapoza 2014).

While China's government and total debt are both rising each year, these figures must be kept in global perspective. According to the IMF, China's government debt is still only 40 per cent of its GDP (2013). For comparison, the government debt-to-GDP ratio in the USA is 104 per cent, in Germany it is 72 per cent, and in Japan it is roughly 243 per cent. In terms of total debt to GDP, which includes the money that is owned by a country's government, banks, businesses, and households, China was at 217 per cent in 2014, while the USA, Germany, and Japan posted figures of 233, 188, and 400 per cent respectively (McKinsey Global Institute 2015).

Other countries' fiscal models cannot be applied to China, as the systems are not comparable. 'It's nothing like the way we think about the United States, because this is in many ways a fake financial system', Andy Rothman remarked in an interview with NPR. To cherry-pick China's municipalities and companies that happen to be losing money and burying themselves in debt is to take a very narrow view of the country's full economic situation. Numerous municipalities, SOEs and lending institutions act as a drain on the system, but many more pump money into it. If one is to talk about Wuhan, Ordos and Wenzhou, one also needs to factor in economically vibrant and profitable cities like Beijing, Shanghai, Shenzhen, Chengdu, Suzhou and Chongqing. A lot of money is being lost in China, but far more is being made.

To put it in simple terms, China has a great deal of money on hand. The country holds over $3.88 trillion in foreign currency reserves, and the People's Bank of China alone is sitting on nearly $700 billion of liquid funds. China has more money on tap than any other country in the world, which would be enough to ride out all but the biggest storm. China's housing market and rampant urbanization are not going to bring down the country's economy or trigger a global meltdown – at least not any time soon. As incredible as it sounds, barring a catastrophic event China will achieve its urbanization ambitions. It's no longer a question of whether China can pull this off; it's already being done.

NINE

What ghost cities become

China's recent urbanization push can be seen as an all-or-nothing gamble on developing an insulated economy that's based on domestic production *and* consumption. It's an initiative to render the local economy more resilient to the ebbs and flows of the global market by making China better able to support itself economically and not rely continually on manufacturing orders from foreign countries. The recessions of 1998 and 2008 left China shuddering, as the degree to which it was dependent on the fruits of an export economy became evident, reliant as this ultimately is on the financial health of the country's top trading partners. A ripple in the West produced a tsunami in China. It therefore became clear that having the bulk of its chips invested in exports was an incredibly insecure long-term economic strategy. To curb the impact that foreign financial downturns can have, China has performed a U-turn and is now looking inward. In 2013, GDP output from China's service sector matched manufacturing for the first time since the start of the economic boom period. The current urbanization push is about continuing in this direction, essentially erecting a massive economic levee around the country, making it more resilient to fluctuations in the global economy.

To this end the country has physically, economically and socially restructured itself. Thousands of villages have been swept off the face of the earth; hundreds of new cities and myriad new towns have taken their place, well in advance of the populations and businesses that are intended to fill them. While many of these are currently lingering in the void between construction and vitalization, the question is rarely if, but rather when. When will these places attract sufficient population and commercial base to function fully?

How long does it take to build and populate a city?

China's urbanization experiment is unlike anything that has been attempted before; there is no model for what is being done. There are no established timelines for the creation and populating of completely new urban centres. All of the new cities, towns and districts that have been heralded as ghost cities in the international media are just that: *new*. Construction on most of them did not even begin until well into the 2000s. Before that, they were mostly rural villages full of cabbage fields and rice paddies. So when discussing Ordos, Zhengdong, Xinyang, Dantu, Meixi Lake, Yujiapu, Nanhui and the other developments investigated in this book, we have to keep in mind that barely a decade ago they didn't even exist. In 2003, the Zhengdong CBD was 3.5 square kilometres of barren lots; yet within five or six years some eighty-six skyscrapers, giant shopping malls, hundreds of apartment buildings, an impressive museum and a world-class theatre were not only built but had been opened to the public and put on the path of vitalization.

Almost all of China's large-scale new cities are currently in the mid-stage of development; some are still construction sites. Every urbanization project in the country has its own timeline. The publicly stated goals regarding final size, GDP and population of new cities are generally set at between eighteen and twenty-two years after construction begins. The PR rap might sound like this:

- By 2020, Nanhui is expected to have 800,000 residents.
- 350,000 people are expected to inhabit Sino-Singapore Tianjin Ecocity by 2023.
- It is projected that 5 million people will live in Zhengdong by 2020.

As Chai Jiliang, the chief publicity officer of Ordos Kangbashi, observed: 'When the construction of Kangbashi began in 2006, we planned to have a town with 300,000 residents by the end of 2020, but it seems that the media doesn't have that much patience' (Wang 2012). When Al Jazeera's Melissa Chan first showed up in Ordos Kangbashi and outed the place as a ghost town, it was a mere five years after construction began. While Wu Haiyong, the deputy director of the Changzhou Housing Administration Bureau, readily admitted that most of the properties on Wuyi Road are empty, he added, 'it is unreasonable to judge the vacancy rate when the area is still in a transition period' (Dong 2013).

Most of China's new cities and districts tend to follow a pattern. For the first few years after the initial central core and some housing is constructed, new developments stand as virtual ghost cities. They are more or less uninhabitable frontier towns, lacking basic essentials such as hospitals, schools, public transportation and highway links. Then they slowly begin to creep forward with added infrastructure, economic activity and culture, as businesses and residents begin trickling in. For a few years the small communities that inhabit these places seem to live rather contentedly, and many claim that they enjoy the 'small town' feel. Eventually, this trickle of residents becomes a flood, and a former outpost of progress, a trendy new district, is swallowed up by the plain old city that it soon becomes.

China's ghost cities are a temporary phenomenon. It is just a phase that new cities move through between construction and vitalization. All too often, China's scantly populated new developments of yesterday become the country's catalysts of growth and progress tomorrow. This is a country that can build large-scale infrastructure with almost unbelievable haste; however, the amount of time it takes to create a living, vibrant urban centre is much longer. Rome wasn't built in a day; neither are new cities in China. On the surface, some new towns may appear ready to support a population – there are buildings, roads, museums, government buildings and parks – but in reality they are not yet habitable. People buy property in these places knowing that it will be quite some time before they will be able – or want – to move in.

It seems rational to conclude that creating a new city is a long-term endeavour that take decades. Nevertheless many foreign journalists and analysts seem to be confused by the vacant sky-scrapers, empty shopping malls and unoccupied housing complexes that dot China's landscape. At first glance these look like failed developments, herds of white elephants spreading over the land, and journalists are quick to declare them as such. They've called them signs of China's overspending catching up with it, the result of irresponsible lending practices, even a nefarious plot to boost GDP or embezzle public funds. While elements of these arguments are often true, the broader analysis has been offered prematurely – the game is at half-time and they're claiming to know the final score. Although it is difficult to believe that

Al Jazeera's Melissa Chan sincerely believed that an entire new city built in the desert of Inner Mongolia should be built and populated within a mere five years, it is almost unfathomable that such a well-known news organization as *60 Minutes* didn't access and use the readily available occupancy and financial data on Zhengdong New District before calling it a ghost city; likewise it is extraordinary that *Business Insider* would publish satellite images of what are obviously half-built urban developments and make a big deal about the fact that they lack residents. This all seems incredibly strange until we reflect that 'crazy' news stories are the ones that get attention, prompt clicks and make money – and perhaps few stories are crazier than a country building hundreds of entirely new cities for nobody. But that story is simply not true.

Not every new city or urban expansion project in China will be successful. Not every patch of countryside will sustain skyscrapers just because they're planted there. Some of these new developments will inevitably fail, fall into ruin and become true ghost towns. New city building is an investment with no guarantee of a return. Yet it's being done on such a massive scale that many projects can fail pitifully without threatening the movement as a whole. Economics is always a big-picture line of study; one cannot isolate a part from the whole and expect it to be an accurate microcosm. Markets are fundamentally made up of excesses and shortages. To measure the vitality of a market one needs to counterbalance failures with successes. One cannot focus on one, ignore the other, and expect it to be an accurate portrayal of reality. Cherry-picking examples of failing new Chinese cities will not give a fair representation of the movement as a whole. Analysts can chide Ordos, Tianjin and Guiyang for manufacturing a city supply that appears to outstretch demand, but without focusing on the many urbanization successes across China the wider context is lost and the critique therefore empty.

By focusing on the extreme and often confusing aspects of China's urbanization movement, the real 'crazy China story' is being missed entirely. In just two decades China has virtually built an entirely new country. Hundreds of new cities have been created and almost every city has been expanded at least twofold. The map has been literally redrawn, populated with little black dots where they have never been before. Most of these new places fill up and we never even hear about them.

Ghost cities epitomize an era of a country inexorably on the rise, but they are inevitably destined to become a forgotten footnote in the long history of China. In a budding but virtually empty new city on the outskirts of Shanghai I asked a young student why there weren't many people there. She looked at me as though I couldn't comprehend the obvious. 'It's a new district', she said, 'it's still under construction. The people come later.' Most new cities and towns in China go through a ghost city phase as they advance slowly through the vitalization process. If given enough time, investment, and sustained attention and favourable policy support from local governments, most of China's large-scale new cities and towns do fill up and become functioning urban centres. Even mighty Pudong was once the object of scorn and jests from foreign reporters as it sat largely empty for years once it appeared to be built. Milton Friedman called it 'a statist monument for a dead pharaoh on the level of the pyramids'. In response to the critics, Mayor Xu Kuangdi said that Pudong was like buying a suit a few sizes too big for a growing boy. Pudong has now grown up: no one calls its CBD a ghost town anymore.

Tiantai

Tiantai's new area is now an inconspicuous outlying section of an inconspicuous small city in the east of China. There is nothing about it that a passer-by would find especially peculiar, and most travellers pass through without retaining a lasting impression. It's a wallpaper town: everybody sees it but there is little memorable to latch onto. In 2006 the place was a ghost town.

Tiantai was where I first came face to face with the reality of China's ghost cities. When I returned eight years later I retraced my steps to the new sector, only to discover that there was no longer anything 'new' about it. I found a neighbourhood of interconnected rows of five-storey buildings that had shops on the ground floor and apartments above. There was a good layer of grime over everything; rust streaks were descending down steel railings, sidewalks were cracked, junk was piled up in front of shops, rickety plastic tables stood outside nondescript restaurants. The businesses were those common to the outskirts of China's cities: rough-looking eating places, prostitution dens, broken-down KTV lounges, dusty convenience stores, as well as places to buy furniture, curtains and random home supplies. A small central square had spaces for street vendors to set up at night and an area for children to play and old people to stroll. Groups of new thirty-storey high-rises were sprouting up on all sides of the neighbourhood now, hemming it in and making it look outdated and old. This part of Tiantai had normalized.

On my first visit the place was deserted; there was just me, and no sounds but my footsteps and the wind. The apartments have now filled up. In the evenings residents return from work and flood the streets. The food pavilions fill up with diners, leaving hardly a greasy plastic lawn table free. Rows of short-skirted prostitutes scurry from windowless vans and quickly file into the pink-lit hair salons that are the front for their illicit trade. Cars move down the streets bumper to bumper. The main

> square is packed with people perusing the stalls of vendors and
> children enjoying carnival rides. There is music, voices, laugh-
> ter, the catcalls of vendors, people yelling into mobile phones,
> the rumbling of engines, the honking of horns – the sounds
> of life everywhere. This is what most of China's ghost cities
> eventually become.

China's urbanization race cannot go on forever. Indeed the white
flags are now being waved announcing the final lap. In September
of 2014, Dong Zuoji, head of the Ministry of Land and Resources,
publicly stated that new guidelines will strictly control new urban
development. Unless a city can prove that its population is too
dense, or some kind of natural disaster occurs, the construction
of new urban districts will be forbidden. This may well signal the
end of an era.

For fifteen years, 2000–2014, China's cities were physically
growing in both size and complexity, but we are now seeing this
movement reach its climax. The high-speed rail network is at an
advanced stage of completion; the new highway system has in large
part been laid; the hundreds of airports that are being built and
expanded are progressing rapidly; the central cores of hundreds
of new cities and urban districts have risen up from the soil. The
process of urbanization has progressed from the testing stage and
is now advancing at full tilt, and the megacity and mega-region
clusters are coming together; the means to increase total energy
output twofold have been set in motion; the housing market is
readjusting and topping out; GDP is stabilizing. Governmental
policies have responded by restricting property speculation while
making other investment options available – thereby scattering the
feeding frenzy. More and more wealthy Chinese individuals and

companies are investing in property abroad and are engaging the array of newly available wealth-management products. China's new city movement has reached the top of the bell curve, and the outward expansion of the country's urban frontiers will soon halt their advance. The next fifteen years will be about filling in the blanks; much of the building has been done, it's now time to do something with it.

The question is no longer whether China will pull off its new city movement. It has already been achieved. The land grabs, evictions and demolitions will continue in the forthcoming decades, but their pace will steadily lessen. Displaced peasants will have children who are fully urban and equipped to deal with life in the city. The culture and traditions of village life will become folklore that recounts the days long ago when the Chinese didn't live all crammed together in identical high-rise apartments in some vertical city or another. We will ride on trains and buses through the outskirts of China's cities never knowing that they were once empty new developments seemingly on the brink of collapse. There will be nothing in the landscape to tell us that just fifteen years before it was all small farms and villages. We will squint through the smog towards the endless horizon of high-rises, skyscrapers and smokestacks and simply assume that it has always been like that.

Bibliography

Alusi, A., Eccles, R., Edmondson, A., and Zuzul, T., 'Sustainable Cities: Oxymoron or the Shape of the Future?', *Harvard Business School,* Working Paper 11-062, 2011.

Amnesty International, 'Houses Demolished without Warning in Beijing', 22 October 2013.

Areddy, James T., 'China's Building Push Goes Underground', *Wall Street Journal,* 10 November 2013.

Atsmon, Yuval, et al., 'Understanding China's wealthy', *McKinsey Quarterly,* July 2009.

Barefoot, Peter, 'Nanchang Homeowners Clash With Forced Demolition Crew', *ChinaSmack.com,* 4 April 2013.

Battaglia, Gabriele, 'Beijing Readies for New Urbanization', *AsiaTimes Online,* 7 August 2013.

Berlin, Joshua, 'With Government Support, China Medical City Looks to Separate Itself from the Pack', *PharmAsia News,* 3 August 2011.

Bloomberg, 'China Debts Dwarf Official Data With Too-Big-to-Finish Alarm', 19 December 2011.

Bloomberg, 'China Cash Squeeze Seen Creating Vietnam-size Credit Hole', 8 July 2013.

Bloomberg, 'China's Ordos Struggles to Repay Debt: Xinhua Magazine', 9 July 2013.

Bloomberg, 'China Coal-fired Economy Dying of Thirst as Mines Lack Water', 24 July 2013.

Bloomberg, 'Top China Banks Triple Debt Write-offs as Defaults Loom', 23 October 2013.

Bloomberg, 'China's Urbanization Loses Momentum as Growth Slows', 25 March 2014.

Bloomberg Businessweek, 'China's Legions of "Housing Slaves"', 28 February 2013.

Brown, Lester, 'China's Water Table Levels Are Dropping Fast', *Grist.org*, 26 October 2001.

Buckley, Chris, 'A Quiet Start to South–North Water Transfer', *New York Times*, 11 December 2013.

Buttimer, Richard J., et al., 'The Chinese Housing Provident Fund', *International Real Estate Review* 7(1) 2004: 1–30.

Carlson, Jack, 'China's Copycat Cities', *Foreign Policy*, 29 November 2012.

Cary, Eve, 'Reforming China's State-Owned Enterprises', *TheDiplomat. com*, 19 June 2013.

Chan, Kam Wing, 'There is No Future as a Labourer; Returning to the Village Has No Meaning', *International Journal of Urban and Regional Research* 34(3) (September 2010): 659–77.

Chan, Melissa, 'China's Empty City', *Al Jazeera*, 10 November 2009.

Chan, Melissa, 'A Wealthy Coal-mining Town in Inner Mongolia, Designed to House One Million People, Remains Nearly Empty, Five Years after Construction Began', *Al Jazeera*, 9 September 2011.

China Economic Review, 'If Beijing is Your Landlord, What Happens When the Lease is Up?', 17 June 2013.

China Economic Review, 'Too Many Central Business Districts, Not Enough Business', 19 March 2014.

Demographia, 'Demographia World Urban Areas: 11th Annual Edition', January 2015.

Dobbs, Richard, et al., 'Urban World: Cities and the Rise of the Consuming Class', McKinsey Global Institute, June 2012.

Dong, Liu, 'Will Ghost Cities Haunt China?', *Global Times*, 30 July 2013.

Dumaine, Brian, 'Rethinking China's cities', *Fortune Magazine*, 3 December 2012.

The Economist, 'Creative Destruction: The Frenzied Pace of Home Demolition May Slow', 30 November 2013.

The Economist, '200% and counting', 16 July 2014.

FlorCruz, Michelle, 'China Property Developer Faces Collapse, Increased "Ghost Cites" Likely', *International Business Times*, 20 March 2014.

Freemark, Yonah, 'Profitable or Not, China Doubles Down on Investments in New Metro Systems', *TheTransportPolitic.com*, 11 September 2012.

Fung, Esther, 'More Than 1 in 5 Homes in Chinese Cities Are Empty, Survey Says', *Wall Street Journal*, 11 June 2014.

Gardels, Nathan, 'Rem Koolhaas: How China Plans to Inhabit Its Future', *Huffington Post*, 12 March 2014.

Guilford, Gwynn, 'A Chinese Housing Market Crash Could Be Even More Disastrous Than America's', *Quartz*, 19 March 2014.

Hartmann, Pascal, 'The Green Delusion', *Architectural Review*, 28 August 2012.

Hsu, Sara, et al., 'The Global Crisis' Impact upon China's Rural Migrants', *Journal of Current Chinese Affairs* 39(2) (2010): 167–85.

International Monetary Fund, 'World Economic Outlook Databases', October 2014.

International Rivers, 'Three Gorges Dam', InternationalRivers.org.

Jackson, John, 'Eathquake Hazards and Large Dams in Western China', *Probe International*, April 2012.

Jiang, Gaoming 'Land Reclamation: Tread Carefully', *ChinaDialogue.net*, 11 March 2008.

Johnson, Ian, 'In China, 'Once the Villages Are Gone, the Culture Is Gone', *New York Times*, 1 February 2014.

Johnson, Ian, 'China Releases Plan to Incorporate Farmers into Cities', *New York Times*, 17 March 2014.

Jones Lang Lasalle, 'Strengthening China's Next Economic Mega-region', August 2014.

Kao, Hang, 'Ghost Cities Springing up near China's First-tier Cities', *Want China Times*, 22 October 2013.

KPMG, 'Zhengzhou Zhengdong New District Investment Environment Study', *KPMG Huazhen*, 2009.

Langfitt, Frank, 'In China's Hugely Indebted Cities, Some Big Bills Are Coming Due', *NPR.org*, 28 January 2014.

Lewis, Charlton, 'China's Great Dam Boom: A Major Assault on Its Rivers', *Yale Environment 360*, e360.yale.edu, 4 November 2013.

Li, Li, 'Not So Paradise Islands', *BeijingReview.com.cn*, 13 February 2012.

Lubin, Gus, 'TIMBER! Home Prices Are Crashing in China's Most Famous Ghost City', *Business Insider*, 6 December 2011.

Lubin, Gus, and Mamta Badkar, 'Scary New Satellite Pictures of China's Ghost Cities', *Business Insider*, 5 March 2013.

Luo Tianyi, et al., 'Majority of China's Proposed Coal-fired Power Plants Located in Water-Stressed Regions', World Resources Institute, 26 August 2013.

Ma, Frank, 'Attractiveness of the New CBDs in Western China', Jones Lang Lasalle, 2 May 2014.

McKinsey Global Institute, 'The Most Dynamic Cities of 2025', 2012.

McKinsey Global Institute, 'Global Cities of the Future: An Interactive Map', June 2012.

McKinsey Global Institute, 'Debt and (Not Much) Deleveraging', February 2015.

Milken Institute, 'China's Housing Market: Is a Bubble about to Burst?', December 2012.

Miller, Tom, *China's Urban Billion*, Zed Books, London, 2012.

Mirviss, Laura, 'Shanghai World Expo Site Transforms', *Architectural Record*, 27 December 2012.

Moore, Malcolm, 'Middle Class Protestors March over World Expo Threat to Shanghai Homes', *Telegraph*, 8 February 2010.

Morris, Ruth, 'Why China Loves to Build Copycat Towns', *BBC News*, 30 June 2013.

New Tang Dynasty Television, 'Activists in Taiwan Protest Shanghai World Expo', 8 April 2010.

Ni, Chun Chun, 'China's Electric Power Industry and Its Trends', Institute of Energy Economics, Japan, April 2006.

Nomura, 'China Affordable Housing Development', June 2011.

Oizumi, Keiichiro, 'Evolution from Mega-Cities to Mega-Regions in China and Southeast Asia', *RIM Pacific Business and Industries* 9(31) 2009.

Oizumi, Keiichiro, 'The Emergence of the Pearl River Delta Economic Zone: Challenges on the Path to Megaregion Status and Sustainable Growth?', *RIM Pacific Business and Industries* 11(41) (2011).

Piew, Pow Choon, and Harvey Neo, 'Eco-cities Need to Be Based around Communities, Not Technology', *ChinaDialogue.net*, 21 October 2013.

Qi, Liyan, 'Fast, Cheap and in the Red: Beijing's Subway System Bled $558 Million Last Year', *Wall Street Journal*, 15 July 2014.

Rabinovitch, Simon, 'China: City Limits', *Financial Times*, 24 June 2013.

Rajagopalan, Megha, 'China to Restrict Expansion of Cities in Move to Curb "Ghost Towns"', Reuters, 26 September 2014.

Ramzy, Austin, 'China's Mountains of Construction Rubble', *New York Times*, 20 October 2013.

Rapoza, Kenneth, 'Following New Loan Default, Is China's Economy Finally on the Brink?', *Forbes*, 21 March 2014.

Rathod, Chandi, and Gus Lubin, 'And Now Presenting: Amazing Satellite Images of the Ghost Cities of China', *Business Insider*, 14 December 2010.

Ren, Shuli, 'Nomura: Why Property Market Is China's No 1 Risk', *Barrons*, 14 March 2014.

Ren, Xuefei, *Urban China*, Polity Press, Cambridge, 2013.

Roach, Stephen, 'China Is Okay', *Project Syndicate*, 29 August 2012.

Ross, John, 'Western Tales of China's Imminent Collapse Are a Bit Rich', *Guardian*, 29 August 2012.

Rothman, Andy, 'China's Property Is Slowing, Not Crashing', *Financial Times*, 1 October 2014.

Ruan, Victoria, 'Li Keqiang Warns of Urbanisation Risks in First Speech as Premier', *South China Morning Post*, 18 March 2013.

Schmitz, Rob, 'In China, a Replica of Manhattan Loses Its Luster', Marketplace.org, 3 July 2013.

Schmitz, Rob, 'Preparing for China's Urban Billion', Marketplace.org, 12 March 2014.

Shao, Xiaoyi, and Koh Gui Qing, 'The Uncomfortable Truth in China's Property Market', Reuters, 6 November 2013.

Shasha, Deng, 'Poorest Chinese Province to Settle 100,000 in New Homes', *Xinhua*, 4 January 2013.

Shih, Mi, 'Making Rural China Urban', *The China Story*, 18 June 2013.

Sigley, Gary, 'Metropole Power: Approaches to Centre and Periphery in Contemporary China', *International Journal of China Studies* 4(2) (August 2013): 177–187.

Southwestern University of Finance and Economics, Chengdu, 'China Household Finance Survey', *Survey and Research Center for China Household Finance*, 6 November 2013.

Su, Jiangyuan, and Li Yao, 'Assisted Relocation Helps Villagers Improve Livelihoods', *China Daily*, 26 March 2013.

Trading Economics, 'China Newly Built House Prices YoY Change 2011–2014', 2014.

UN News Center, 'UN Pavilion Launches at World Expo 2010 in Shanghai', 1 May 2010.

UN Watch, '38 Rights Groups Urge U.N. to Investigate Shanghai Expo Eviction of 18,000 Families', 22 July 2010.

Visser, Robin, *Cities Surround the Countryside*, Duke University Press, Durham NC, 2010.

Wang, Kaihao, 'Kangbashi Thrives Despite Perceptions', *China Daily*, 24 December 2012.

Wang, Yue, 'Chinese Minister Speaks out against South–North Water Diversion Project', *Forbes*, 20 February 2014.

Want China Times, 'Plot Sold for Record 450% Premium in Shanghai's Lingang New City', 22 December 2013.

Wei, Qian, 'Removing Mountains', *NewsChinaMag.com*, April 2013.

Wei, Tan, 'Business Hubs in Doubt', *Beijing Review*, 2005.

Wells, Paul, 'China Postscript: Ghost Town, pop. 13 million', *MacLean's Magazine*, 16 February 2012.

Wilson, David, 'Monoclonals in China', Trade Secrets Blog, Nature.com, 1 April 2011.

Wilson, David, 'Chinese Bureaucracy', Trade Secrets Blog, Nature.com, 6 May 2011.

Wong, Edward, 'Pollution Rising, Chinese Fear for Soil and Food', *New York Times*, 30 December 2013.

World Bank, 'Cost of High Speed Rail in China One Third Lower Than in Other Countries', 10 July 2014.

Xiao, Bin, 'It Takes Brains and Guts', *China Daily*, 19 August 2003.

Xie, Liangbing, and Tian Yan, 'Supersizing Small Cities in China', *Economic Observer*, 14 May 2013.

Xinhua, 'Chinese Government Net Assets at 55.3 trl Yuan: Research', *Xinhua*, 20 December 2014.

Yanfeng, Qian, 'China Must Replace Half Its Homes in 20 Years – Report', *China Daily*, 7 August 2010.

Yang, Jian, 'China's River Pollution "a threat to people's lives"', *Shanghai Daily*, 17 February 2012.

Yishi, Zhu, 'Crowded Shandong Grabs Sea for Future Growth', *Caixin*, 20 September 2011.

Yue, Wang, 'China Unlikely to Reduce Coal Use in the Next Decade', ChinaDialogue.net, 10 February 2014.

Yue, Zhang, et al., 'How to Spot a Fake Eco-city', ChinaDialogue.net, 25 August 2011.

Yung, Chester, 'China's Ghost Cities to Get Spookier', *Wall Street Journal*, 16 May 2014.

Zhang, Dingmin, and Bonnie Cao, 'China Cities May Tighten Property Curbs as Slowdown Lifts Target', Bloomberg, 30 July 2013.

Zhang, Ming'ai, 'China to Create 10 More City Clusters', China.org.cn, 12 July 2013.

Zhao, Shuqing, et al., ' China's Environmental Challenges: The Way Forward', *Frontiers in Ecology and the Environment* 4(7) September 2006: 341–6.

Zhou, Joe, 'What Makes China's New CBDs Successful in the Long Term?', Jones Lang Lasalle, 21 May 2012.

Zhou, Kate, *China's Long March to Freedom,* Transaction Publishers, New Brunswick NJ, 2011.

Index

National Audit Office, 189
National Bureau of Statistics, 167, 184, 186
National Development and Reform Commission, 5
National Science Department, Terminology Committee, 39
Neo, Harvey, 125
Netease, news portal, 14
new cities (*xinshi*), 6, 44, 50, 65; downtown cores, 67; ghost city phase, 201–2; mid-stage development, 198; project cities, 82; speculation, 80; universities, 75, 77; vitalizing process, 66
new districts (*xinqu*), 44; population density, 61
New South China Mall, Dongguan, 192–4
new towns, 44–5, 93
New York, CBD, 134
Ningbo, CBD, 135
Nomura, 174, 178
Nu River, 162

Oizumi, Keiichiro, 87
One City, Nine Towns Initiative, Shanghai, 83, 93, 106
Ordos Kangbashi, Inner Mongolia, 3, 67–8, 78, 196–9, 201; debt, 190; GDP per capita, 73; Museum, 72

parallel migrations, 51
Pearl River, 166; Delta, 36, 71, 88, 141, 152, 192
Peking University, 174
per capita disposable income, rise, 185
Pow Choon Piew, 125
Poyang Lake, 165, 167; shrinkage, 166
prefectures, authority transfer, 42
Probe International, 164
property 'bubble', 63–4; laws, 13; market, 57; market fiscal system, 174; seizures, 25; speculation, 79; tax, 179
Pudong, 77, 100, 202; Lujiazui Central Business District, 9, 134

Qingdao, Shandong province, 143
Qing dynasty, 36, 150; fall of, 118
Qiu Baoxing, 15, 117

real estate: GDP significance, 188; speculation, 176; status, 178; status indicator, 175
relocation propaganda, 21
Ren, Xuefei, *Urban China*, 136
Renmin University, 24, 33
rental yield, low, 58
reservoirs, pollution build-up, 164
Roach, Stephen, 48
Rothman, Andy, 190, 195
rural counties, phasing out, 43
rural land, *hukou* swap, 27

Sanya, Hainan Island, 37; refacing of, 25
saving, incentive lack, 183
'scape', 90
Semple, David, 186,
Shandong province, 75, 161
Shanghai, 51, 59, 62, 95, 111–15, 117, 119, 141, 167, 186, 196; absentee homeowners clampdown, 80; China Pavilion, 11; Dachang township, 75; Expo site, 9–12; high-speed train, 110; Hongqiao, 81; housing cost, 174; investment magnet, 113; Lujiazui CBD, 137–8; Master Plan 1999, 92; mega-region, 88; Metro, 76, 96; 'middle-class utopia', 93; Nanhui New Town, 37; New Netherlands Town, 100–101; One City, Nine Towns programme, 83, 93, 106; '1–9–9–6' plan, 92, 105; outskirts, 91; population expansion, 41; Pudong/CBD District, 49, 74, 132, 135; real-estate market, 63; refacing of, 25; shanty towns, 88–9; size 40, 92; suburbanization, 121; University new campus, 56, 76; Yangshan Deep Water Port, 37
Shantou, 37
shanty towns, 87; Shanghai, 88, 89
Shanxi, 71